Modern Critical Interpretations

Charlotte Brontë's
Jane Eyre

Modern Critical Interpretations

Modern Critical Interpretations

Charlotte Brontë's
Jane Eyre

Edited and with an introduction by
Harold Bloom
Sterling Professor of the Humanities
Yale University

Chelsea House Publishers
NEW YORK ◇ PHILADELPHIA

© 1987 by Chelsea House Publishers, a subsidiary of
Haights Cross Communications.

Introduction © 1986 by Harold Bloom

Printed and bound in the United States of America

10   9

∞ The paper used in this publication meets the minimum
requirements of the American National Standard for
Permanence of Paper for Printed Library Materials,
Z39.48–1984.

Library of Congress Cataloging-in-Publication Data
Charlotte Brontë's Jane Eyre.
    (Modern critical interpretations)
    Bibliography: p.
    Includes index.
    1. Brontë, Charlotte, 1816–1855.   Jane Eyre.
I. Bloom, Harold.   II. Series.
PR4167.J33C4   1986   823'.8   86–17613
ISBN 0–87754–731–9

Contents

Editor's Note

This book brings together a representative selection of the best criticism devoted to Charlotte Brontë's *Jane Eyre,* arranged here in the chronological order of its original publication. I am grateful to Jennifer Wagner for her erudition and judgment in helping me to edit this volume.

My introduction emphasizes the novel's Byronic ethos, as well as what must be regarded as Charlotte Brontë's vengeance upon Byron, at once her literary precursor and her idealized erotic object. W. A. Craik begins the chronological sequence with an overview of the structural unity of the book, a unity found in Brontë's masterly handling of setting, plot development, and time. In an exegesis of what she calls the novel's "dogmatic form," Barbara Hardy, comparing the novel to *Robinson Crusoe,* questions its moral continuity, finding that Jane's "choice comes from grace rather than from a continuity of moral and spiritual habit."

The Marxist critic Terry Eagleton valiantly attempts to demystify *Jane Eyre* as a structure that merges "bourgeois initiative and genteel settlement, . . . spiritual equality and social distinction" into a purely "mythical unity." This differs sharply from Helene Moglen's equally brave effort to see the novel as "the creation of a feminist myth."

Tracing what they call "plain Jane's progress," Sandra M. Gilbert and Susan Gubar read the novel as Jane Eyre's quest for self-strengthening, for making herself the equal of the world that Rochester represents. Rosemarie Bodenheimer also views Jane Eyre as a quester in search of her own story, a story that rewrites Rochester's idea of Jane into terms all her own.

In this book's final essay, Margaret Homans portrays Jane Eyre as rejecting the literalization of the metaphor that would make nature the mother and Jane her child. The heroine thus "can resist nature's appeal that she become part of the literal," a resistance that would divest Jane of all male literalizations of female status and role, whether in a fiction or in society.

Introduction

I

The three Brontë sisters—Charlotte, Emily Jane, and Anne—are unique literary artists whose works resemble one another's far more than they do the works of writers before or since. Charlotte's compelling novel *Jane Eyre* and her three lesser yet strong narratives— *The Professor, Shirley, Villette*—form the most extensive achievement of the sisters, but critics and common readers alike set even higher the one novel of Emily Jane's, *Wuthering Heights,* and a handful of her lyrical poems. Anne's two novels—*Agnes Grey* and *The Tenant of Wildfell Hall*—remain highly readable, although dwarfed by *Jane Eyre* and the authentically sublime *Wuthering Heights.*

Between them, the Brontës can be said to have invented a relatively new genre, a kind of northern romance, deeply influenced both by Byron's poetry and by his myth and personality, but going back also, more remotely yet as definitely, to the Gothic novel and to the Elizabethan drama. In a definite, if difficult to establish sense, the heirs of the Brontës include Thomas Hardy and D. H. Lawrence. There is a harsh vitalism in the Brontës that finds its match in the Lawrence of *The Rainbow* and *Women in Love,* though the comparison is rendered problematic by Lawrence's moral zeal, enchantingly absent from the Brontës' literary cosmos.

The aesthetic puzzle of the Brontës has less to do with the mature transformations of their vision of Byron into Rochester and Heathcliff, than with their earlier fantasy-life and its literature, and the relation of that life and literature to its hero and precursor, George Gordon, Lord Byron. At his rare worst and silliest, Byron has nothing like this scene from Charlotte Brontë's "Caroline Vernon," where Caroline confronts the Byronic Duke of Zamorna:

The Duke spoke again in a single blunt and almost coarse sentence, compressing what remained to be said, "If I were a bearded Turk, Caroline, I would take you to my harem." His deep voice as he uttered this, his high featured face, and dark, large eye burning bright with a spark from the depths of Gehenna, struck Caroline Vernon with a thrill of nameless dread. Here he was, the man Montmorency had described to her. All at once she knew him. Her guardian was gone, something terrible sat in his place.

Byron died his more-or-less heroic death at Missolonghi in Greece on April 19, 1824, aged thirty-six years and three months, after having set an impossible paradigm for authors that has become what the late Nelson Algren called "Hemingway all the way," in a mode still being exploited by Norman Mailer, Gore Vidal, and some of their younger peers. Charlotte was eight, Emily Jane six, and Anne four when the Noble Lord died and when his cult gorgeously flowered, dominating their girlhood and their young womanhood. Byron's passive-aggressive sexuality—at once sadomasochistic, homoerotic, incestuous, and ambivalently narcissistic—clearly sets the pattern for the ambiguously erotic universes of *Jane Eyre* and *Wuthering Heights*. What Schopenhauer named (and deplored) as the Will to Live, and Freud subsequently posited as the domain of the drives, is the cosmos of the Brontës, as it would come to be of Hardy and Lawrence. Byron rather than Schopenhauer is the source of the Brontës' vision of the Will to Live, but the Brontës add to Byron what his inverted Calvinism only partly accepted, the Protestant will proper, a heroic zest to assert one's own election, one's place in the hierarchy of souls.

Jane Eyre and Catherine Earnshaw do not fit into the grand array of heroines of the Protestant will that commences with Richardson's Clarissa Harlowe and goes through Austen's Emma Woodhouse and Fanny Price to triumph in George Eliot's Dorothea Brooke and Henry James's Isabel Archer. They are simply too wild and Byronic, too High Romantic, to keep such company. But we can see them with Hardy's Tess and, even more, his Eustacia Vye, and with Lawrence's Gudrun and Ursula. Their version of the Protestant will stems from the Romantic reading of Milton, but largely in its Byronic dramatization, rather than its more dialectical and subtle analyses in Blake and Shelley, and its more normative condemnation in Coleridge and in the Wordsworth of *The Borderers*.

II

The Byronism of Rochester in *Jane Eyre* is enhanced because the narrative is related in the first person by Jane Eyre herself, who is very much an overt surrogate for Charlotte Brontë. As Rochester remarks, Jane is indomitable; as Jane says, she is altogether "a free human being with an independent will." That will is fiercest in its passion for Rochester, undoubtedly because the passion for her crucial precursor is doubly ambivalent; Byron is both the literary father to a strong daughter, and the idealized object of her erotic drive. To Jane, Rochester's first appearance is associated not only with the animal intensities of his horse and dog, but with the first of his maimings. When Jane reclaims him at the novel's conclusion, he is left partly blinded and partly crippled. I do not think that we are to apply the Freudian reduction that Rochester has been somehow castrated, even symbolically, nor need we think of him as a sacrificed Samson figure, despite the author's allusions to Milton's *Samson Agonistes.* But certainly he has been rendered dependent upon Jane, and he has been tamed into domestic virtue and pious sentiment, in what I am afraid must be regarded as Charlotte Brontë's vengeance upon Byron. Even as Jane Eyre cannot countenance a sense of being in any way inferior to anyone whatsoever, Charlotte Brontë could not allow Byron to be forever beyond her. She could acknowledge, with fine generosity, "that I regard Mr. Thackeray as the first of modern masters, and as the legitimate high priest of Truth; I study him accordingly with reverence." But *Vanity Fair* is hardly the seedbed of *Jane Eyre,* and the amiable and urbane Thackeray was not exactly a prototype for Rochester.

Charlotte Brontë, having properly disciplined Rochester, forgave him his Byronic past, as in some comments upon him in one of her letters (to W. S. Williams, August 14, 1848):

Mr. Rochester has a thoughtful nature and a very feeling heart; he is neither selfish nor self-indulgent; he is ill-educated, misguided; errs, when he does err, through rashness and inexperience: he lives for a time as too many other men live, but being radically better than most men, he does not like that degraded life, and is never happy in it. He is taught the severe lessons of experience and has sense to learn wisdom from them. Years improve him; the effervescence of youth foamed away, what is really good in him still remains. His nature is like wine of a good vin-

tage, time cannot sour, but only mellows him. Such at
least was the character I meant to portray.

Poor Rochester! If that constituted an accurate critical summary,
then who would want to read the novel? It will hardly endear me to
feminist critics if I observe that much of the literary power of *Jane
Eyre* results from its authentic sadism in representing the very masculine Rochester as a victim of Charlotte Brontë's will-to-power over
the beautiful Lord Byron. I partly dissent, with respect, from the
judgment in this regard of our best feminist critics, Sandra M. Gilbert and Susan Gubar:

> It seems not to have been primarily the coarseness and sex-
> uality of *Jane Eyre* which shocked Victorian reviewers . . .
> but . . . its "anti-Christian" refusal to accept the forms,
> customs, and standards of society—in short, its rebellious
> feminism. They were disturbed not so much by the proud
> Byronic sexual energy of Rochester as by the Byronic
> pride and passion of Jane herself.

Byronic passion, being an ambiguous entity, is legitimately
present in Jane herself as a psychosexual aggressivity turned both
against the self and against others. Charlotte Brontë, in a mode between those of Schopenhauer and Freud, knows implicitly that Jane
Eyre's drive to acknowledge no superior to herself is precisely on the
frontier between the psychical and the physical. Rochester is the out-
ward realm that must be internalized, and Jane's introjection of him
does not leave him wholly intact. Gilbert and Gubar shrewdly observe that Rochester's extensive sexual experience is almost the final
respect in which Jane is not his equal, but they doubtless would agree
that Jane's sexual imagination overmatches his, at least implicitly.
After all, she has every advantage, because she tells the story, and
very aggressively indeed. Few novels match this one in the author's
will-to-power over her reader. "Reader!" Jane keeps crying out, and
then she exuberantly cudgels that reader into the way things are, as
far as she is concerned. Is that battered reader a man or a woman?
I tend to agree with Sylvère Monod's judgment that "Charlotte
Brontë is thus led to bully her reader because she distrusts him . . .
he is a vapid, conventional creature, clearly deserving no more than
he is given." Certainly he is less deserving than the charmingly
wicked and Byronic Rochester, who is given a lot more punishment

than he deserves. I verge upon saying that Charlotte Brontë exploits the masochism of her male readers, and I may as well say it, because much of *Jane Eyre*'s rather nasty power as a novel depends upon its author's attitude towards men, which is nobly sadistic as befits a disciple of Byron.

"But what about female readers?" someone might object, and they might add: "What about Rochester's own rather nasty power? Surely he could not have gotten away with his behavior had he not been a man and well-financed to boot?" But is Rochester a man? Does he not share in the full ambiguity of Byron's multivalent sexual identities? And is Jane Eyre a woman? Is Byron's Don Juan a man? The nuances of gender, *within literary representation,* are more bewildering even than they are in the bedroom. If Freud was right when he reminded us that there are never two in a bed, but a motley crowd of forebears as well, how much truer this becomes in literary romance than in family romance.

Jane Eyre, like *Wuthering Heights,* is after all a romance, however northern, and not a novel, properly speaking. Its standards of representation have more to do with Jacobean melodrama and Gothic fiction than with George Eliot and Thackeray, and more even with Byron's *Lara* and *Manfred* than with any other works. Rochester is no Heathcliff; he lives in a social reality in which Heathcliff would be an intruder even if Heathcliff cared for social realities except as fields in which to take revenge. Yet there is a daemon in Rochester. Heathcliff is almost nothing but daemonic, and Rochester has enough of the daemonic to call into question any current feminist reading of *Jane Eyre.* Consider the pragmatic close of the book, which is Jane's extraordinary account of her wedded bliss:

> I have now been married ten years. I know what it is to live entirely for and with what I love best on earth. I hold myself supremely blest—blest beyond what language can express; because I am my husband's life as fully as he is mine. No woman was ever nearer to her mate than I am; ever more absolutely bone of his bone and flesh of his flesh.
>
> I know no weariness of my Edward's society: he knows none of mine, any more than we each do of the pulsation of the heart that beats in our separate bosoms; consequently, we are ever together. To be together is for us to

be at once as free as in solitude, as gay as in company. We talk, I believe, all day long: to talk to each other is but a more animated and an audible thinking. All my confidence is bestowed on him, all his confidence is devoted to me; we are precisely suited in character—perfect concord is the result.

Mr. Rochester continued blind the first two years of our union: perhaps it was that circumstance that drew us so very near—that knit us so very close! for I was then his vision, as I am still his right hand. Literally, I was (what he often called me) the apple of his eye. He saw nature—he saw books through me; and never did I weary of gazing for his behalf, and of putting into words the effect of field, tree, town, river, cloud, sunbeam—of the landscape before us; of the weather round us—and impressing by sound on his ear what light could no longer stamp on his eye. Never did I weary of reading to him: never did I weary of conducting him where he wished to go: of doing for him what he wished to be done. And there was a pleasure in my services, most full, most exquisite, even though sad—because he claimed these services without painful shame or damping humiliation. He loved me so truly that he knew no reluctance in profiting by my attendance: he felt I loved him so fondly that to yield that attendance was to indulge my sweetest wishes.

What are we to make of Charlotte Brontë's strenuous literalization of Gen. 2:23, her astonishing "ever more absolutely bone of his bone and flesh of his flesh"? Is *that* feminism? And what precisely is that "pleasure in my services, most full, most exquisite, even though sad"? In her "Farewell to Angria" (the world of her early fantasies), Charlotte Brontë asserted that "the mind would cease from excitement and turn now to a cooler region." Perhaps that cooler region was found in *Shirley* or in *Villette,* but fortunately it was not discovered in *Jane Eyre.* In the romance of Jane and Rochester, or of Charlotte Brontë and George Gordon, Lord Byron, we are still in Angria, "that burning clime where we have sojourned too long—its skies flame—the glow of sunset is always upon it—."

The Shape of the Novel

W. A. Craik

The shape of [*Jane Eyre*] is very much represented by the places where the action occurs, which Charlotte Brontë makes an essential part of the structure, as well as the atmosphere, of her stories. Places have indeed as much character as people, and serve many of the same purposes, a use which *Jane Eyre* shares with *Wuthering Heights,* or, to name a later novelist, Hardy. They operate by accurately and vividly selected detail, and often on more than one level. Just as a single person is felt and judged in different ways at the same time, so places may arouse a variety of conflicting feelings, and the tensions, beginning fairly simply with the child's view of Gateshead, increase in complexity through Lowood, Thornfield, Morton, and Ferndean. Gateshead is plainly a place of torment, the house of the Reeds, where all the rooms are places of cold and dread, whether in company or isolation; even in the nursery Jane cannot touch the dolls' house furniture "for the tiny chairs and mirrors, the fairy plates and cups were [Georgiana's] property" (chap. 4), and the windows are fretted with "frost-flowers." Jane's only pleasures there are melancholy, uncertain, fleeting, and solitary: the vignettes in Bewick,

> The rock standing up alone in a sea of billow and spray; the broken boat stranded on a desolate coast; the cold and ghastly moon glancing through bars of cloud at a wreck just sinking.
>
> (chap. 1)

From *The Brontë Novels.* © 1968 by W. A. Craik. Methuen, 1968.

are a brilliant choice: Bewick's vignettes do arouse such feelings, so Jane's reactions seem authentic. Bessie's kindness, represented by "a tart on a certain brightly painted china plate, whose bird of paradise, nestling in a wreath of convolvuli and rosebuds, had been wont to stir in me a most enthusiastic sense of admiration" (chap. 3), is, when she obtains it, "like most other favours long deferred and often wished for, too late! I could not eat the tart: and the plumage of the bird, the tints of the flowers, seemed strangely faded" (ibid.). Yet these pleasures remain with Jane: Bewick can be clearly seen as an influence on the visionary paintings Jane does at Lowood and shows Mr Rochester at Thornfield: the pleasure in brilliant artefacts inspires her admiration for

> a very pretty drawing-room, and within it a boudoir, both spread with white carpets, on which seemed laid brilliant garlands of flowers; both ceiled with snowy mouldings of white grapes and vine-leaves, beneath which glowed in rich contrast crimson couches and ottomans; while the ornaments on the pale Parian mantel-piece were of sparkling Bohemian glass, ruby red; and between the windows large mirrors repeated the general blending of snow and fire.
>
> (chap. 11)

—which Mr Rochester later dismisses (with reason):

> "The glamour of inexperience is over your eyes," he answered; "and you see (Thornfield) through a charmed medium: you cannot discern that the gilding is slime and the silk draperies cobwebs; that the marble is sordid slate, and the polished woods mere refuse chips and scaly bark."
>
> (chap. 20)

reproducing thus the movement of the earlier passage about the plate.

Lowood is physically hard and aesthetically repulsive. A reader's immediate recollections of it are of burnt porridge, "a strong steam redolent of rancid fat," "a keen north-east wind, whistling through crevices of our bedroom windows all night long, [that] had made us shiver in our beds, and turned the contents of the ewers to ice" (chap. 6), girls "in brown stuff frocks of quaint fashion, and long holland pinafores" (chap. 5), whose hair is not allowed to curl, even naturally. But the pleasures are more mature and more extensive. Sensuous pleasure remains; in food for the famished such as Miss Temple's supper ("How fragrant was the steam of the beverage, and the scent of the toast," and that ever memorable "good-sized seed-cake" [chap. 8]); and in the scenery ("prospects of noble summits girdling a great hill-hollow, rich in verdure and shadow; a bright beck, full of dark stones and sparkling eddies" [chap. 9]). It is also the place of congenial companionship—Miss Temple, Helen Burns, and even Mary Ann Wilson; and intellectual pleasures are added—of drawing, learning French, and conversing with Miss Temple.

Such simple combinations of good and bad prepare for the much more subtle use of Thornfield. The place has several aspects: freedom and happiness are embodied in some parts of the house, in its gardens, and in the surrounding landscape; while the sinister and evil are embodied in the upper storeys (especially at night); the grand world of society, heartless and tasteless, belongs in the drawing room. These are all directly related to Jane's association with Mr Rochester, and help us to feel the moral weight of what happens. Jane first meets Mr Rochester outside, in Hay Lane; he tells her about Céline in the cold wintry garden, standing outside the house as he is standing, mentally, outside his own experiences and coldly assessing them; after Mason has been attacked and departed, Mr Rochester sits in the garden in summer sunrise with Jane, reviewing in the dawn of his new emotions the painful and violent ones of his youth, which link so closely with what has just happened inside the house; he proposes to Jane in the garden, in the orchard on Midsummer-eve, where all is "Eden-like" and as he said before "all is real, sweet and pure" (chap. 20). The proposal is unlawful, but its spirit is not, and the setting of it cannot fail to make us feel so. By contrast what happens indoors is ambiguous or evil. When she has just met Mr Rochester, Jane, returning from Hay in the evening and loitering outside, sees the house as a "grey hollow filled with rayless cells" (chap. 12); the suggestion of prison and place of the dead continues: Bertha Mason is shut up on the third floor, and when she escapes, setting fire to Mr Rochester's bed, visiting Jane and tearing her veil, and setting fire finally to Jane's room, all she does is done indoors and upstairs. Downstairs the Gothic terror is replaced by vapid society and the pressure it exerts on Jane and Mr Rochester: he can only half-communicate with her, "in mortal dread of some prating prig of a servant passing" (chap. 17), or disguised as a gipsy, and as soon as they enter the hall after the proposal, Mrs Fairfax, "pale, grave, and amazed" (chap. 23), recalls us to the standards of society, Thornfield is precious because Jane has "lived in it a full and delightful life" (ibid.); but it is insubstantial and doomed to perish, representing the falsity that must be burned away by suffering before Jane and Mr Rochester can come together, and that Jane's dreams of it as a crumbling ruin foreshadow (chap. 25).

Moor House is in many ways its antithesis: the building is a symbol of security and family unity, a place Jane can "care for" in the most practical sense, as the "cleaning down" process with Hannah proves (chap. 34). It provides Jane with a family and a function, but subjects her to more anxiety than Thornfield ever did, when St John calls her to submit to a soulless and self-destroying marriage of duty. To read about Moor House reproduces Jane's experiences there: it is both less absorbing than Thornfield, and a great deal more trying. On the other hand, Moor House and Jane's life there gain dignity, power, and health from the surrounding hill-country. Moorland comforts her in her flight:

> Beside the crag, the heath was very deep: when I lay down my feet were buried in it; rising high on each side, it left only a narrow space for the night-air to invade. I folded my shawl double, and spread it over me for a coverlet; a low, mossy swell was my pillow.
>
> (chap. 28)

It is also a fitting background for St John, a stern setting for his stern proposals, which are made high in the hills where

> the mountain shook off turf and flower, had only heath for raiment, and crag for gem—where it exaggerated the wild to the savage, and exchanged the fresh for the frowning—where it guarded the forlorn hope of solitude, and a last refuge for silence.
>
> (chap. 34)

(The reader's mind recalls the hills round Lowood, the "noble summits" which also provided a setting both for suffering, when "mists chill as death wandered to the impulse of east winds along those purple peaks" [chap. 9], and for a new companionship and intellectual growth.) Jane's schoolteacher's cottage—one-up, one-down—offers a contrast to Thornfield (the bare necessities of life, physical, mental, and emotional), just as the moorland landscape offers a noble but barren contrast to the fertile country round Thornfield:

> A little room with white-washed walls, and a sanded floor; containing four painted chairs and a table, a clock, a cupboard, with two or three plates and dishes, and a set of tea-things in delf.
>
> (chap. 31)

Here are merely the essentials for physical life, to correspond with the meagre mental life offered by teaching ignorant farmgirls; the setting makes one understand how Jane can say, "I felt desolate to a degree. I felt . . . degraded," and then, in the next paragraph, be thankful to be "a village schoolmistress, free and honest, in a breezy mountain nook in the healthy heart of England" (chap. 31).

The story ends at Ferndean Manor, about thirty miles from Thornfield, "quite a desolate spot," "deep buried in a wood" in an "ineligible and unsalubrious site," with "dank and green decaying walls" (chaps. 36 and 37). Though the house and its milieu obviously provide a new setting for what is to be a new relationship, a setting in harmony with a meeting where "rapture is kept well in check by pain" (chap. 37), they are not relevant in the same way as the others have been, since they contrast with the present action, rather than reveal it. Although Jane does not tell us, we can safely assume that once married, she and Mr Rochester leave so unhealthy and gloomy a place, where it is difficult to accommodate even one guest. The house and its setting as seen at the beginning of chapter 37 present the epitome of what Mr Rochester has suffered and become in the last year; and as soon as possible, on the morning after her arrival, Jane leads Mr Rochester "out of the wet and wild wood into some cheerful fields" (ibid.) where "the flowers and hedges looked refreshed" by the "sad sky, cold gale, and small penetrating rain" of the night before, just as his sufferings have at last brought new life to Mr Rochester.

Thus the various sections of the story have a moral and artistic relevance to the main action and to each other which helps to prevent any feeling that the book has a broken back. The story is unified also in ways more obviously structural. Innumerable threads of association and construction link section to section and incident to incident; and Charlotte Brontë creates proportioned emphasis, subtle parallels, and a sense of layers of simultaneous action to her basically

linear story. The mere proportion of space occupied plays a large part
in suggesting relative importance to the reader: four chapters for
Gateshead, six for Lowood, fifteen for Thornfield (interrupted by a
single very long chapter when Jane returns to Gateshead); one long
chapter for her suffering and starvation, seven for Morton, and three
for Ferndean. Within the Thornfield period there is only one chapter
before Mr Rochester appears, twelve chapters for the courtship
(more than is spent on anything else in the novel), but also two very
long ones which cover the span between the wedding and Jane's
flight. It can clearly be seen that the narrative movement runs against
the natural passage of time, but nevertheless time and the hour run
through the roughest day. References to season and weather, and
even dates and days of the week, are frequent and exact as well as
atmospheric: the intervals of time between Jane's arrival at Thornfield in October and Mr Rochester's proposal on Midsummer Eve
are carefully noted, and equally accurate are those between her midsummer agony on the moors, St John's news of her fortune brought
on a snowy November the fifth, and her return to Ferndean on a wet
Thursday summer evening (the third of June). Jane does not live
wholly in the present (as fictional characters so often do) but is always aware of her own past and possible future—she imagines with
frightening truth what marriage to St John would entail—and she
recognizes death as an accepted fact for others and herself:

> I laughed at him as he said this. "I am not an angel," I
> asserted; "and I will not be one till I die: I will be myself."
>
> (chap. 24)

The single long chapter in the middle of the Thornfield episode,
when Jane revisits Gateshead and Mrs Reed dies, is probably the
finest example of Charlotte Brontë's sure sense of shape. This chapter (21) covers the space of a month (May), the month immediately
after the dreadful night when Mason is attacked, and the summer
dawn when Mr Rochester almost tells Jane about his marriage and
almost proposes to her. The next main event, two weeks after her
return, is his real proposal. No one can fail to feel that the emotional
effect of the interruption and return is right, but the reasons why
Charlotte Brontë takes such a risk as to break off here, when things
between Jane and Mr Rochester are clearly reaching a culmination,
are not immediately clear.

The most obvious and mechanical reason why Jane returns is to hear Mrs Reed's deathbed confession telling her of the uncle to whom she will owe both the breaking off of her wedding and also her fortune. It is much more organically a culmination of what has gone before, and an anticipation of what is to come. The culmination is necessary because Jane is to return to Thornfield to face the two greatest emotional experiences of her life: Mr Rochester's and her own mutual declarations, and her renunciation of him. For these to have their full power we must see Jane as a whole being, a part of all that she has met, moulded to this experience by all that has happened to her hitherto. The return to Gateshead recreates her childhood and its sufferings, and charts her moral and emotional growth. Georgiana and Eliza can no longer oppress her, and of Mrs Reed she can say, and we can believe:

> I had left this woman in bitterness and hate, and I came back to her now with no other emotion than a sort of ruth for her great sufferings, and a strong yearning to forget and forgive all injuries.

> (chap. 21)

The episode is equally vital as anticipation and preparation in perhaps more separate ways. It separates Mr Rochester's proposal from the scenes which have led up to it, and sets it apart from them. Jane, away from Mr Rochester and Thornfield for the first time, shows no weakly conventional or self-indulgent pain at the temporary separation; we are therefore the more ready to credit her extreme agony when she is forced to leave for good. So utterly unsentimental a handling of death prepares for the equally unsentimental love and agony to come:

> A strange and solemn object was that corpse to me. I gazed on it with gloom and pain: nothing soft, nothing sweet, nothing pitying, or hopeful, or subduing, did it inspire; only a grating anguish for *her* woes—not *my* loss—and a sombre tearless dismay at the fearfulness of death in such a form.

> (chap. 21)

Gateshead and its affairs have reached a climax, which prepares for the even greater climax to come. As a climax, it is the antithesis of Mr Rochester's proposal; dreadful and unfeeling, it moves us and Jane, so that we are moved even more by the intense happiness which follows. Jane's power to hate intensely and to express it, recalled here, presupposes that her love and its expression will be equally intense. The episode puts before us distinctions we shall have to make at Morton, where "judgment untempered by feeling" (ibid.) will again be offered, but in a more subtle guise, as religious renunciation. A view of life is created in which death takes a realistic place, so that when Bertha Mason dies, this convenient event seems not improbable, since four (Helen Burns, John Reed, his mother, and the West Indian uncle) have died before her.

Within the larger individual sections of the action, the movement varies, but Charlotte Brontë tends always to work in terms of the big scene, completely realized and dramatically presented. She likes to use the effect of shock on her reader, but she never loses her emotional continuity; she therefore moves from one big scene to the next, by a variety of methods: the smaller (but significant) intermediate scene, the pause for Jane's reflection and analysis of what has passed, and, very rarely, the juxtaposition of sharply contrasting important scenes. She is also careful to provide proper preparation where shock is unsuitable; and the prefatory material, though of various kinds, is always concerned with building up the right associations, or recalling the necessary personalities. The result is a wave-like movement, with a drawing-back between each surge of an incoming tide. Attention to continuity descends even to the nice placing of chapter divisions. The most interesting place to examine her structural methods is where they are at their finest and most sustained, that is, during the fifteen chapters chronicling the events at Thornfield. These move by a series of exciting, even sensational, events, seen in entirety. The sense of shock is as much in the material as the presentation, and Charlotte Brontë never cheats by cutting a scene off short to get her excitement. The first of these big scenes is the one where Mr Rochester falls off his horse in Hay Lane (chap. 12), but this is unmistakably being underplayed, partly to gain power in retrospect, and partly so as to keep plenty of power in reserve. Mr Rochester is at this point, as Jane says, "only a traveller taking the short cut to Millcote." There must, after all, be no suggestion of falling in love at first sight—though this is what Mr Rochester almost does: "It was well that I had learnt that this elf must return to me—that it belonged to my house down below—or I could not have felt it pass away from under my hand, and seen it vanish behind the dim hedge, without singular regret" (chap. 12). Thereafter Charlotte

Brontë has a good deal to do in the way of establishing relationships, and filling in past history, which all prevents action. But immediately this is done, the movement begins in chapter 15, with the fire, the very night after Mr Rochester has told Jane about Céline Varens. The next is the first evening Jane and Adèle meet the house party (chap. 18), where Jane suffers her social inferiority, Mr Rochester's flirtation with Blanche, and finally Mr Rochester's all too perceptive questions; the charade comes next (chap. 18), then the fortune-telling gipsy (chap. 19), then the dreadful night when Mason is attacked, and the tête-à-tête in the orchard at dawn which follows (chap. 20); then at last (after Mrs Reed's death and the very brief scene where Jane meets Mr Rochester in Hay Lane again) the proposal at midsummer (chap. 23). These chapters form an entity. The scenes are splendidly varied: there is the passionate tête-à-tête after the fire, and the disguised one of the fortune-telling; there are scenes when Mr Rochester makes the advances (the fire, his few words in the hall, his confession in the orchard when Mason has left), and scenes where Jane does (the proposal itself, and the little scene in Hay Lane preceding it); there are scenes where others are the real actors, and the relevance is in the emotions Jane feels (the "polite" conversations about governesses, and the charade), scenes where the action is shared (Mason's terrible night). They take place at night, and by day, indoors and out (and not arbitrarily, for the setting is always significant); but however they occur, whoever is concerned, and wherever and whenever they happen, they each sweep things a little nearer to that Midsummer Eve in the orchard. After them comes another movement, whose motive is foreboding, which works in terms of fantasy and illusion, where dreams seem more real than life, where an ecstatic daylight reality runs alongside frightening omens at night, which coalesce after the abortive wedding, and culminate when Jane tears herself away from Thornfield. Similarly the chapters at Morton move by way of various excitements and pressures until Jane hears Mr Rochester's voice and breaks free from St John.

The transitions between these scenes are as varied as the scenes themselves, and equally superb. We never feel that Charlotte Brontë is having to summon her resources, or rest between engagements. The action has all the continuity of real life, and the interest never slackens. What goes on in between the events absorbs us just as much as the events themselves, since our eye never leaves what absorbs us most—Jane herself—though *her* eye of course may wander very considerably. Hence the variety in the interludes. These are generally a pause for breath, and for reassessment. The day after the fire is a fine example of Charlotte Brontë's method, involving in a short space a number of the devices she employs. After the fire Jane cannot sleep, and admits to us and herself for the first time how she feels about Mr Rochester—not yet explicitly but in images:

> Till morning dawned I was tossed on a buoyant but unquiet sea, where billows of trouble rolled under surges of joy . . . [but] a counteracting breeze blew off land, and continually drove me back. Sense would resist delirium: judgment would warn passion.
>
> (chap. 15)

The following day (chap. 16) bears out what she says. The first incident is the servants Leah and Grace Poole putting the bedroom to rights, sense and the light of common day taking over the scene of delirium. Grace in person de-romances herself, with her "pint of porter and bit of pudding" (chap. 16). Having left her, Jane tries to explain Mrs Poole's position to herself: Mr Rochester may once have put himself in her power; they are the same age: "she may possess originality and strength of character to compensate for the want of personal advantages. Mr Rochester is an amateur of the decided and eccentric." Jane's reasoning is quite sensible, and even more sensible is the way she rejects the hypothesis when she considers Mrs Poole in person. The passage has an extra layer of significance, since all the points which make her reasoning sound here point to herself, not Mrs Poole, as the partner for Mr Rochester, as Jane herself recognizes. At this point Jane's thoughts again impinge upon action:

> I was now in the schoolroom; Adèle was drawing; I bent over her and directed her pencil. She looked up with a sort of start.
>
> "Qu'avez-vous donc, mademoiselle?" said she; "Vos doigts tremblent comme la feuille, et vos joues sont rouges: mais, rouges comme des cerises!"
>
> "I am hot, Adèle, with stooping!" She went on sketching, I went on thinking.
>
> (ibid.)

The day ends with conversation between Jane and Mrs Fairfax at tea, with the same kind of external manifestation of feeling:

"You must want your tea," said the good lady, as I
joined her; "you ate so little at dinner. I am afraid," she
continued, "you are not well today: you look flushed and
feverish."

(ibid.)

and the conversation reveals that Mr Rochester has left, and that the
events are about to take a new course, with the arrival of the house
party and Blanche. Jane accepts this check to her feelings, and sup-
plements it by contrasting herself with Blanche and drawing the two
portraits. The whole interlude is "sense" resisting "delirium":

When once more alone, I reviewed the information I had
got; looked into my heart, examined its thoughts and feelings, and endeavoured to bring back with a strict hand
such as had been straying through imagination's boundless
and trackless waste, into the safe fold of common sense.

(ibid.)

The use of incident as well as thought demonstrates at the same time
that her conduct is always ruled by this sense, and that her feelings
are so powerful as to break through the restraint she imposes on
herself; the conclusion to the chapter drives home its point and directs us forward to what is to happen next:

Ere long, I had reason to congratulate myself on the course
of wholesome discipline to which I had thus forced my
feelings to submit: thanks to it, I was able to meet subsequent occurrences with a decent calm; which, had they
found me unprepared, I should probably have been unequal to maintain, even externally.

(ibid.)

As the action at Thornfield sweeps itself forward speed gathers,
the intervals between scenes get shorter and less obtrusive. After
Jane's dreadful night with Mason, her talk with Mr Rochester in the
orchard immediately follows. The events of the month of courtship
rush on upon another without pause, and make their own comment
on themselves, so Jane need interpose no more than

My future husband was becoming to me my whole world;
and more than the world: almost my hope of heaven. He
stood between me and every thought of religion, as an
eclipse intervenes between man and the broad sun. I could

not, in those days, see God for his creature: of whom I had made an idol.

(chap. 24)

We are swept forward to the disaster at the altar, on past Mr Rochester's public admission, into his confession and persuasion of Jane; their agonizing battle of wills, from one startling revelation to the next, and have no pause to breathe until Jane gets into the coach which leaves her at Whitcross;

> Gentle reader, may you never feel what I then felt! May your eyes never shed such stormy, scalding, heart-wrung tears as poured from mine. May you never appeal to Heaven in prayers so hopeless and so agonized as in that hour left my lips: for never may you, like me, dread to be the instrument of evil to what you wholly love.

(chap. 27)

Since Charlotte Brontë's method is in many ways a dramatic one, she uses a good deal of dialogue. *Jane Eyre* has the advantage over *Villette* and *The Professor* that its characters (all except Adèle and Sophie) are English-speaking. Charlotte Brontë has a fine ear for characteristic idioms of class and age, which the deliberate and obvious artificiality of the house party dialogues tends to obscure. She moves in a narrow compass, making little use of dialect, having no character to compare with Emily Brontë's Joseph; Hannah, the only really broad speaker, is generally reported, and her direct speech gets its flavour from idiom rather than pronunciation:

> "Are you book-learned?" she inquired presently.
> "Yes, very."
> "But you've never been to a boarding-school."
> "I was at a boarding-school eight years."
> She opened her eyes wide. "Whatever cannot ye keep yourself for, then?"

(chap. 29)

The idiom of the respectable servant is precisely caught, whether in Leah, Grace Poole, Bessie, or Robert Leaven here:

> "And how is Bessie? You are married to Bessie?"
> "Yes, Miss: my wife is very hearty, thank you; she brought me another little one about two months since—

we have three now—and both mother and child are thriving."

"And are the family well at the House, Robert?"

"I am sorry I can't give you better news of them, Miss: they are very badly at present—in great trouble . . . Mr John died yesterday was a week, at his chambers in London."

(chap. 21)

Mrs Fairfax (whatever the actual or ostensible date of the book) goes back a generation or more, and her idiom recalls Jane Austen. Dialogue between Jane and others, especially Mr Rochester, performs many functions besides verisimilitude: it is often not naturalistic, yet it almost always convinces, and always has a flavour of its own. Like the speech in *Wuthering Heights* it is often quite literally unspeakable, and is, despite its dramatic method, quite unlike that of a play or of life.

Charlotte Brontë's style is like no one else's. This is generally agreed and immediately obvious. Being odd, it has often been called bad, by those who have preconceived notions of what a novelist's style should be, and in particular a Victorian lady novelist's. But as Mr Rochester says in another context, "unheard-of combinations of circumstances demand unheard-of rules" (chap. 14). Both Charlotte Brontë and Emily found this to be so in their writing; both solved their own problem in their own way, and while Charlotte occasionally allows herself to copy other novelists (the voice heard most frequently besides her own is that of Thackeray, whom she greatly admired), her best effects are always her most individual ones. Again the distinction must be made between Charlotte Brontë and her creation Jane Eyre. While Jane has many of Charlotte Brontë's characteristics, it is clear that what she says is almost always "in character," and Charlotte Brontë's success is so complete that it is only noticeable in her occasional failures, where an idiom is heard that we recognize from *Shirley* or *Villette*:

Women are supposed to be very calm generally: but women feel just as men feel; they need exercise for their faculties, and a field for their efforts as much as their brothers do; they suffer from too rigid a restraint, too absolute a stagnation, precisely as men would suffer; and it is narrow-minded in their more privileged fellow-creatures to say that they ought to confine themselves to making puddings and knitting stockings, to playing on the piano and embroidering bags. It is thoughtless to condemn them, or laugh at them, if they seek to do more or learn more than custom has pronounced necessary for their sex.

(chap. 12)

I know poetry is not dead, nor genius lost; nor has Mammon gained power over either, to bind or slay: they will both assert their existence, their presence, their liberty and strength again one day. Powerful angels, safe in heaven! They smile when sordid souls triumph, and feeble ones weep over their destruction. Poetry destroyed? Genius banished? No! Mediocrity, no; do not let envy prompt you to the thought. No; they not only live, but reign, and redeem: and without their divine influence spread everywhere, you would be in hell—the hell of your own meanness.

(chap. 32)

Both these jar by being generalizations, and being divorced from the topic, though the one is meditative and the other rhetorical. Generally, however, Charlotte Brontë's expression is determined by the speaker, by the occasion, by the emotional content of what is being said, or by the atmosphere of the episode, always bearing in mind that everything that is not spoken by one of the other characters is, whatever else it is doing, being used to express Jane.

With *Jane Eyre* Charlotte Brontë establishes what the novel is to be and do in her hands, and has found her course between what she herself summarized as the "real" and the "true," between which she was confused in *The Professor*.

Providence Invoked: Dogmatic Form in *Jane Eyre* and *Robinson Crusoe*

Barbara Hardy

There must be many novels where Providence is invoked to mark the successful resolution of difficulties, as in the conclusion of Smollett's *Roderick Random* and *Peregrine Pickle,* for instance, but Defoe, both in *Robinson Crusoe* and other novels, uses Providence not as a convenient *deus ex machina* in a story of little religious interest, but as an informing principle. When we come to the nineteenth century the concept of Providence is plainly outworn and discredited, and we find Dickens, George Eliot, and Meredith defining the egocentric or mercenary character by evoking just that faith in a *special* Providence which is taken for granted in Defoe. Podsnap, Casaubon, and Harry Richmond are examples of faith in discredited Providence, and this devaluation has an interesting place in novels which explore the responsibility and conflict of individuals and social relations. But in one of the most interesting early Victorian novels, *Jane Eyre,* Providence is still very much alive. The dubious moral implication of egocentricity and material profit are gone but the formal implications remain much the same. Providence is not a dead word when used by Charlotte Brontë, and it is no accident that she wrote that Providence had decreed her marriage with Arthur Nicholls and wrote a novel which is structurally very like *Robinson Crusoe.* There is the same rising intonation of optimistic faith, the same pattern of prayer and answer, and a very similar intercession of dreams, portents, and

From *The Appropriate Form: An Essay on the Novel.* © 1964, 1970 by Barbara Hardy. Northwestern University Press, 1971.

coincidences. *Jane Eyre,* however, is not a novel about religious conversion, and perhaps this is to be regretted.

Jane is like Crusoe in her disregard of Heaven. What he puts first is adventure, what she puts first is human love. Her early passionate sense of injustice is rebuked by Helen Burns, who refers her to the approval of conscience and the kingdom of spirits and warns her, "You think too much of the love of human beings." Although Jane's conversion to Helen's values is cursorily treated, and indeed taken for granted in her discovery of value and activity as pupil and teacher at Lowood, by the time she comes to leave we have reached the second stage of the action, where prayer is substituted for the demand for justice.

Like Robinson Crusoe, Jane finds that prayer always meets a practical response, and the relationship of prayer and answer is an important thread in the action. She prays first for liberty but feels the prayer "scattered on the wind," so—testifying to the discipline she tells us she has acquired—she substitutes the prayer for "a new servitude" and thinks hard about ways and means. The answer is playfully dramatized as an internal colloquy, but in the full context of the novel there are other implications:

> A kind fairy, in my absence, had surely dropped the required suggestion on my pillow; for as I lay down it came quietly and naturally to my mind: "Those who want situations advertise; you must advertise in the *Herald.*"
>
> (chap. 10)

The practical answers of Providence return in Jane's crisis. The vision recalls her painting of the Evening Star—moonlit, vapourish, glorious-browed, shining in the blue—and speaks to the spirit as the painted vision had been seen by the spirit, saying, "My daughter, flee temptation." Later, alone and hungry on the moor, reenacting Bessie's hymn which is an important source for feeling, image, and situation, she asks again, "Oh, Providence, sustain me a little longer! Aid—direct me!" The "false light" of the hymn has been left behind, and what now appears as an *ignis fatuus* is in fact the light of her cousin's house. As Kathleen Tillotson notes in her analysis of the theme in *Novels of the Eighteen-Forties,* coincidence is the symbol of Providence. St John speaks to Jane when she has reconciled herself to death and asserted her faith, "Let me try to wait his will in silence." Finally her appealing prayer receives a direct answer when she is tempted to accept her cousin's proposal and is saved by hearing Rochester's voice. This is the conversation of her prayer and Rochester's, for his cry to her has been the response to her prayer: "Show me, show me the path!" and her response to him has answered his prayer, now that he has become capable of prayer like Crusoe, after punishment and repentance.

> I asked of God, at once in anguish and humility, if I had not been long enough desolate, afflicted, tormented. . . . That I merited all I acknowledged—that I could scarcely endure more, I pleaded; and the alpha and omega of my heart's wishes broke involuntarily from my lips in the words "Jane! Jane! Jane!"
>
> (chap. 37)

It is only after Rochester too has been converted and has repented that Providence can join their prayers as human question and answer, and reconcile the human and the divine, reason, conscience, and passion.

Kathleen Tillotson argues convincingly that Jane's converse with the invisible world gives the novel its moral unity which makes us accept her decision as inevitable. This unity is not entirely an individual one, but is rather imposed from without, like the pattern of *Robinson Crusoe*. And the unity of theme is only one aspect of unity. This is not to deny that the novel is animated and individual: Jane's conflict between discipline and passion for instance, before the great choice comes up, is delicately and plausibly dramatized in her defensive teasing and sparring, as well as being individualized and generalized in her relations with her aunt and cousins, and with her second set of cousins. To say that the novel is defined by an external doctrine is not to deny its realism, and we have only to compare it with stereotyped religious novels like those of Elizabeth Sewell or Charlotte Yonge, good enough of their kind, to see the superior subtlety of Charlotte Brontë's psychology and imagination. The moral pattern of the novel can be simply described, in terms of the conflict between human love and heavenly faith, passion and reason, rather as Mr Rochester's phrenological fortune-telling expresses it, as the conflict in which reason reins feeling, judgement overrules passions and desires, wind, earthquake, and fire are succeeded by the still small voice of conscience. The psychological detail and personality of that conflict, within Jane and externalized in other characters, are not simply schematic. The Providential form allows for some free play of human relationships, both at their best, in Jane's own history and development, and at their weakest, in the traces of Angrian fantasy in Rochester's character and marriage and in the conclusion. There are places in the novel when this Providential form is a source not of unity but disintegration.

This weakness is by no means easy to pinpoint, since it is a defect in belief rather than a straightforward literary lapse, though it is the literary consequences of belief which concern me most in this discussion. Both *Robinson Crusoe* and *Jane Eyre* are novels whose action relies on supernatural machinery and in each case it is not the artifice of fantasy but the fantasy of belief, which determines the movement and the motivation. In *Robinson Crusoe*, however, a much more persistently religious novel, there is no gap between realism and fantasy, and the fantastic explanation is merely one way of interpreting the material. Robinson Crusoe's dreams and voices appear at every crisis, but the crisis and its results are explicable in rational terms. When he dreams of rescuing a savage victim, it is a likely happening. When he decides not to hail the English longboat, he gives good reasons for not doing so. When he decides to travel by land from Portugal he is remembering past storms and shipwrecks. When he gives up the brewing project, it is explained as impracticable, because of the lack of yeast. It may be that the premise of the novel, his long survival in solitude, is explicable only in terms of his repentance and expiation, but this is the premise, scarcely to be challenged, and the handling of time and the constant sense of energetic reflection and activity give us no strained sense of plausibility. There are, moreover, the hysterical moments when the need for human company asserts itself wildly. Although the Providential form determines the action, there is a constant realistic explanation and accompaniment which makes it much more than religious fantasy.

In *Jane Eyre* the religious explanation determines motive and action in what is a more insistent and consistent fashion. And yet there is a gap in the novel which seems to be the result of its ideological pattern. This gap is one which may not be apparent to readers sharing Charlotte Brontë's beliefs, since they, like Charlotte Brontë, may be able to assume that faith is the product of growth and education. It is this assumption which allows the novelist to show two distinct stages in Jane's feelings and beliefs and leave the middle stage of transition undramatized. Yet it is a vital part of the novel's causality.

Jane is shown as passionate and intelligently rational. She begins with a need for love and self-respect and suffers aggression, rejection, and humiliation. Helen Burns puts her finger on Jane's "excessive" need for human love and it is significant that Jane meets her friend's unquestioning faith with doubts and questions. When Helen confronts the sense of outrage with "Love your enemies," Jane replies that this is impossible. When Helen on her deathbed affirms her faith and tells Jane, "I am going to God," Jane asks, "Where is God? What is God?" and, "You are sure that there is such a place as heaven; and that our souls can get to it when we die?" She thinks to herself, "Where is that region? Does it exist?"

We come to see that Jane achieves a rational discipline, and the tacit disappearance of her sense of outrage is acceptable enough as a consequence of maturity, especially since she has at Lowood found both affection and self-respect. We are not surprised when she forgives her aunt. This is an intelligible adult act of feeling which the child could not have achieved. What we do not come to see is exactly how Jane comes to accept Helen Burns's faith, even though such faith is at the root of her decision to leave Rochester. She has presumably moved away from her early doubts about Heaven by the time she comes to see her dying aunt, and her doubts are now of a different kind, about the actual destination of her aunt's spirit: "Whither will that spirit—now struggling to quit its material tenement—flit when at length released?" There is an explicit reminder of Helen's deathbed, but our attention is not drawn to Jane's change in belief. She still speaks of *Helen's* beliefs. Her moment of affirmation comes with her moral crisis and test, not before it, and she then affirms her need for dignity and self-respect, fully backed by the preceding action, and her faith that the "invisible world" is impelling her towards the renunciation of Rochester. She has told us earlier that her love for Rochester "stood between her and every thought of religion" but the actual growth of that religious feeling is the one thing the novel takes for granted and does not demonstrate. Every other detail in their courtship and conflict has roots which can be traced back to the beginnings. Her rejection of his extravagant gifts is entirely in keeping with her sense of dependence and memories of humiliation, and her hard-won independence and dignity comes out convincingly in her relations with the Ingrams, her wary pride as she keeps Rochester at a distance, and the characteristic flash, during her great moral conflict, when she remembers his cast-off mistresses and—prudently if unfairly—distrusts him. It is this pride and common sense which assert themselves at the time of choice. The religious argument is bound to be less convincing outside her faith just because Charlotte Brontë seems to have found it unnecessary to include religious development in the otherwise full and detailed account of Jane's growth. I am aware that her contemporary readers may have found it easier to share the undemonstrated assumption, but George Eliot's lack of moral sympathy with the novel, for instance, may well be explained by this incompleteness.

The question and answer of Jane's moral debate speaks in two voices, the voice of Christian law and the voice of personal prudence. Her love pleads for Rochester and indiscreetly flouts Jane's self-respect by asking, "Who in the world cares for *you?* or who will be injured by what you do?" The answer is conventionally Christian in its content, but its tone is that of the child who complained so bitterly of injustice and humiliation, sharpened now by the experience of dignity and status, strengthened by rational detachment:

> Still indomitable was the reply—"*I* care for myself. The more solitary, the more friendless, the more unsustained I am, the more I will respect myself. I will keep the order given by God; sanctioned by man."
>
> (chap. 27)

Yet this is far from being a novel where we can ignore the religious references and observe only the psychological development. After Jane discovers that Rochester is already married she longs to die and there is only one sign of life: "One idea only still throbbed lifelike within me—a remembrance of God." We feel, I suggest, less that this one lifelike idea is the inevitable strength of a demonstrated faith, less that she would be violating a law which we have seen her learn in the course of her struggles, than that she is saved by the intervention of God.

It is true, as Kathleen Tillotson argues, that if Jane did not resist Rochester and the strong plea of love, "the moral pattern of the novel would be violated." I do not think, however, that the moral pattern is one which fully informs the dramatic psychology of the novel. In places it is taken for granted and not given proper emphasis. My distinction is perhaps plainer if we compare Jane's conflict and choice with that of Maggie Tulliver. Maggie rejects Stephen, and in most ways her position is easier than Jane's, since she would violate no actual divine or man-made *law* by marrying him. In other ways it is more difficult, since she faces injury to Lucy and Philip, whereas Jane is placed in the isolated position where she can hurt no one but herself. The distinction between breaking a commandment or a law, and hurting other people, is not the vital one here. There is the other important distinction, which I am trying to bring out, between an internally established and dramatized morality and an ideological assumption. Maggie acts and reasons in the clear context of her need for love and her ability to love, from her theoretical and untested self-abnegation. We feel that her motives are psychologically and morally unified, and whether we agree with her decision or not, there is no doubt about the moral continuity of the novel. Jane acts and reasons from precepts which have been presented strongly in Helen Burns, and much less emphatically in Jane herself. We have not seen the process of her religious education and faith, and the divine law which she invokes in the crisis has not been associated with either her feelings or her reason. Her choice comes from grace rather than from a continuity of moral and spiritual habit. The distinction is indicated by Charlotte Brontë herself, when Helen Burns tells Jane not to rely on her "feeble self, or . . . creatures feeble as you." Robinson Crusoe has to be checked in self-reliance and private enterprise. George Eliot's characters have only their "feeble selves" and their relationships with their fellows. Jane's *character* seems to demonstrate the strength of the individual and human relationships, but the *action* demonstrates the need for heavenly resources.

George Eliot rejected *Jane Eyre* not simply for the reason I have suggested, but also because she disapproved of the divorce laws, though she had not yet broken the commandment Jane keeps: "All self-sacrifice is good—but one would like it to be in a somewhat nobler cause than that of a diabolical law which chains a man soul and body to a putrefying carcase" (*The George Eliot Letters,* ed. Gordon S. Haight). I do not think the weakness of the moral pattern lies in the nature of Jane's decision, or in Charlotte Brontë's silence on the subject of divorce law. Its weakness comes from imposing an ideology on to a realistic psychological pattern. The comparison with *Robinson Crusoe* should make it plain that I am using the word "imposed" in a precise sense. Both novels show a belief in divine intercession and dramatize the workings of heavenly power and grace. I am not objecting to *Jane Eyre* because it expresses the belief that motivation is more than a personal and social matter but because it delineates faith in a rather muffled fashion. George Eliot shows action as determined by a mixture of social causes, moral and psychological habit, human influence, and chance. At some points she even suggests a Providential cause, as in *Silas Marner* or at the end of *The Mill on the Floss,* but never within a moral conflict. Defoe and Charlotte Brontë make the Providential intervention crucial, both in action and conflict. *Robinson Crusoe* combines the hero's development with the ways of God in a way which has none of the strains of Charlotte Brontë's complex story, where the actual relations and conflict of Jane and Rochester could be seen quite independently of the Providential pattern, at least up to their parting. But the action depends largely on that pattern, in its coincidences and its final outcome. The framework of the novel is consistently Providential, but within the frame there are omissions and simplifications. I suggest that we should not hasten to condemn Charlotte Brontë for writing out of neurotic fantasy nor praise her for moral consistency and sound psychology without examining the ways in which the ideology informs the novel as a whole.

It is the ideological assumption which makes it possible for the fantasy to work, both in the destruction of Rochester and in the happy ending. Whether or not we agree with Richard Chase that the dominant pattern is that of domesticated myth—"the tempo and energy of the universe can be quelled, we see, by a patient, practical woman"—we should surely observe the importance of the Providential form. Chase observes that the universe is "chastened by an assertion of will," and says that after the blinding of Rochester "The universe, not previously amenable to supernatural communication between the parted lovers, now allows them to hear each other though they are leagues apart." The universe is acting in a coherent and consistent manner, for it is Providence answering Rochester's prayer after confession and expiation. We may well observe that his actual conversion is even less elaborated than Jane's, and once again it is a pattern of action and change imposed from without, grace rather than organic process, which determines and completes the story.

Jane Eyre: A Marxist Study

Terry Eagleton

Helen Burns, the saintly schoolgirl of *Jane Eyre,* has an interestingly ambivalent attitude to the execution of Charles I. Discussing the matter with Jane, she thinks "what a pity it was that, with his integrity and conscientiousness, he could see no farther than the prerogative of the crown. If he had but been able to look to a distance, and see to what they call the spirit of the age was tending! Still, I like Charles—I respect him—I pity him, poor murdered king! Yes, his enemies were the worst: they shed blood they had no right to shed. How dared they kill him!"

Helen's curious vacillation between a coolly long-headed appreciation of essential reformist change and a spirited Romantic conservatism reflects a recurrent ambiguity in the novels of Charlotte Brontë. It is an ambiguity which shows up to some extent in Helen's own oppressed life at Lowood school: she herself, as a murdered innocent, is partly the martyred Charles, but unlike Charles she is also able to "look to a distance" (although in her case towards heaven rather than future history), and counsel the indignant Jane in the virtues of patience and long-suffering. That patience implies both a "rational" submission to the repressive conventions of Lowood (which she, unlike Jane, does not challenge), and a resigned endurance of life as a burden from which, in the end, will come release.

The problem which the novel faces here is how Helen's kind of

From *Myths of Power: A Marxist Study of the Brontës.* © 1975 by Terry Eagleton. Barnes & Noble Books, 1975.

self-abnegation is to be distinguished from the patently canting version of it offered by the sadistic Evangelical Brocklehurst, who justifies the eating of burnt porridge by an appeal to the torments of the early Christian martyrs. Submission is good, but only up to a point, and it is that point which Charlotte Brontë's novels explore. Jane's answer to Brocklehurst's enquiry as to how she will avoid hell—"I must keep in good health, and not die"—mixes childish naiveté, cheek and seriousness: "*I* had no intention of dying with him," she tells Rochester later. And indeed she doesn't: it is mad Bertha who dies, leaving the way clear for Jane (who has just refused St John Rivers's offer of premature death in India) to unite with her almost martyred master. Helen Burns is a necessary symbol, but her career is not to be literally followed. When she smiles at the publicly chastised Jane in the Lowood classroom, "It was as if a martyr, a hero, had passed a slave or victim, and imparted strength in the transit." That conjunction of "martyr" and "hero" is significant: martyrdom is seen as both saintly self-abnegation and heroic self-affirmation, a realisation of the self through its surrender, as the name "Burns" can signify both suffering and passion. But Helen, who fails to keep in good health and dies, symbolises in the end only one aspect of this desirable synthesis, that of passive renunciation. Like Jane, she triumphs in the end over tyrannical convention, but unlike Jane that triumph is achieved through her own death, not through someone else's.

Where Charlotte Brontë differs most from Emily is precisely in this impulse to negotiate passionate self-fulfilment on terms which preserve the social and moral conventions intact, and so preserve intact the submissive, enduring, everyday self which adheres to them. Her protagonists are an extraordinarily contradictory amalgam of smouldering rebelliousness and prim conventionalism, gushing Romantic fantasy and canny hard-headedness, quivering sensitivity and blunt rationality. It is, in fact, a contradiction closely related to their roles as governesses or private tutors. The governess is a servant, trapped within a rigid social function which demands industriousness, subservience and self-sacrifice; but she is also an "upper" servant, and so (unlike, supposedly, other servants) furnished with an imaginative awareness and cultivated sensibility which are precisely her stock-in-trade as a teacher. She lives at that ambiguous point in the social structure at which two worlds—an interior one of emotional hungering, and an external one of harshly mechanical necessity—meet and collide. At least, they do collide if they are not wedged deliberately apart, locked into their separate spheres to forestall the disaster of mutual invasion. "I seemed to hold two lives," says Lucy Snowe in *Villette,* "the life of thought, and that of reality; and, provided the former was nourished with a sufficiency of the strange necromantic joys of fancy, the privileges of the latter might remain limited to daily bread, hourly work, and a roof of shelter." It is, indeed, with notable reluctance that Lucy is brought to confess the existence of an inner life at all: at the beginning of the novel she tells us, in a suspiciously overemphatic piece of assertion, that "I, Lucy Snowe, plead guiltless of that curse, an overheated and discursive imagination"—and tells us this, moreover, in the context of an awed reference to ghostly haunting. Her response to the "ghost" who flits through Madame Beck's garden is unwittingly comical in its clumsy lurching from romance to realism:

> Her shadow it was that tremblers had feared through long generations after her poor frame was dust; her black robe and white veil that, for timid eyes, moonlight and shade had mocked, as they fluctuated in the night-wind through the garden-thicket.
> Independently of romantic rubbish, however, that old garden had its charms.

It is a splitting of the self common in Charlotte's novels: Caroline Helstone in *Shirley* feels herself "a dreaming fool," unfitted for "ordinary intercourse with the ordinary world"; and William Crimsworth of *The Professor,* slaving away as an underpaid clerk, finds little chance to prove that he is not "a block, or a piece of furniture, but an acting, thinking, sentient man."

To allow passionate imagination premature rein is to be exposed, vulnerable and ultimately self-defeating: it is to be locked in the red room, enticed into bigamous marriage, ensnared like Caroline Helstone in a hopelessly self-consuming love. Passion springs from the very core of the self and yet is hostile, alien, invasive; the world of internal fantasy must therefore be locked away, as the mad Mrs Rochester stays locked up on an upper floor of Thornfield, slipping out to infiltrate the "real" world only in a few unaware moments of terrible destructiveness. The inner world must yield of necessity to the practical virtues of caution, tact and observation espoused by William Crimsworth—the wary, vigilant virtues by which the self's lonely integrity can be defended in a spying, predatory society, a society on the watch for the weak spot which will surrender you into its hands. The Romantic self must be persistently recalled to its deliberately narrowed and withered definition of rationality. "Order! No snivel!—no sentiment!—no regret! I will endure only sense and resolution," whispers Jane Eyre to herself, fixing her errant thoughts on the hard fact that her relationship with Rochester is of a purely cash-nexus kind.

In the end, of course, it isn't. With the ambiguous exception of *Villette,* the strategy of the novels is to allow the turbulent inner life satisfying realisation without that self-betraying prematureness which would disrupt the self's principled continuity—a continuity defined by its adherence to a system of social and moral convention. The tactic most commonly employed here is the conversion of submissive conventionalism itself from a mode of self-preservation to a mode of conscious or unconscious self-advancement. Mrs Reed's remark to Jane in the red room—"It is only on condition of perfect submission and stillness that I shall liberate you"—is triumphantly validated by the novel: it is Jane's stoical Quakerish stillness which captivates Rochester. Her refusal to act prematurely for her own ends both satisfies restrictive convention and leads ultimately to a fulfilling transcendence of it. Rochester would not of course find Jane attractive if she were merely dull, but neither would he love her if, like Blanche Ingram, she were consciously after his money. Jane must therefore reveal enough repressed, Blanche-like "spirit" beneath her puritan exterior to stimulate and cajole him, without any suggestion that she is, in Lucy Snowe's revealing words about herself, "bent on success." Jane manages this difficult situation adroitly during their courtship, blending flashes of flirtatious self-assertion with her habitual meek passivity; she sees shrewdly that "a lamb-like submission and turtle-dove sensibility" would end by boring him. She must demonstrate her quietly self-sufficient independence of Rochester as a way of keeping him tied to her, and so, paradoxically, of staying tied to and safely dependent on him. That this involves a good deal of dexterous calculation—calculation which, if pressed too far, would seriously undermine Jane's credibility as a character—should be obvious enough: it is not, perhaps, wholly insignificant that Rochester's comment to Jane in the original manuscript—"coin one of your wild, shy, provoking smiles"—is misprinted in the first edition as "wild, *sly,* provoking smiles." If Rochester recognises Jane intuitively as a soul mate, so after all does St John Rivers, who tells her that his ambition is unlimited, his desire to rise higher insatiable, and his favoured virtues "endurance, perseverance, industry, talent." Rivers must of course be rejected, as reason rather than feeling is his guide, and Jane's career can only culminate successfully when "feeling" can be "rationally" released; feeling without judgement, she muses, is "a washy draught indeed," but judgement without feeling is "too bitter and husky a morsel for human deglutition." Even so, there is more than a superficial relationship between Rivers, a rationalist with feverishly repressed impulses, and Jane's own behaviour: in her case, too, "Reason sits firm and holds the reins, and she will not let the feelings burst away and hurry her to wild chasms." Not prematurely, anyway, and certainly not to early death in India.

Jane, then, must refuse Rivers as she has refused Rochester: loveless conventionalism and illicit passion both threaten the kind of fulfilment the novel seeks for her. Yet of course Rivers represents more than mere convention. In his fusion of disciplined aloofness and restless desire he is an extreme version of Jane herself, akin to her in more than blood; and he is acute enough to spot the affinity: "for in your nature is an alloy as detrimental to repose as that in mine; though of a different kind." The difference, however, is what finally counts. It is true that Jane finds Rivers's restlessness intriguing as well as alarming: the "frequent flash and changeful dilation of his eye," his "troubling impulses of insatiate yearnings and disquieting aspirations," evoke crucial aspects of herself at the same time as they recall Rochester's engaging moodiness. Indeed, Rivers's repressed love for Rosamund Oliver is a cruder, more agonised version of Rochester's own early enigmatic relationship with Jane. Yet Rivers is a frigid as well as a Romantic figure, and for Jane to accept him would mean disastrous compromise. "I daily wished more to please him: but to do so, I felt daily more and more that I must disown half my nature, stifle half my faculties, wrest my tastes from their original bent, force myself to the adoption of pursuits for which I had no natural vocation."

Half her nature is significant. Rivers is not to be dismissed out of hand, since like Rochester he images aspects of Jane's fractured self which must not be denied. Both men are also attractive in a more subtle sense: each lives out a different kind of deadlock between passion and convention, suffering and affirmation, and so projects Jane's own predicament in more dramatic style. Rochester, an oppressed younger son of the gentry, has suffered at the hands of social convention and so like Jane has a history of deprivation; but unlike her he has achieved worldly success, cuts a glamorous figure in county society, and so blends social desirability with a spice of thwarted passion and an underdog past. His cool attempt to violate the marriage conventions suggests a cavalier stance towards the code which governs Jane, and so, while naturally condemned by her, displays the flamboyant mastery she finds alluring in him because it is absent in herself. At the same time, however, his bigamous scheme is a pathetically abortive rebellion against the stringent pressures of orthodoxy, and so stirs Jane's sympathetic fellow-feeling. The act confirms his superiority to Jane while showing what they have in common, brings him within emotional reach without damage to the dominative style which makes him worth reaching for. Rivers, by contrast, is unconventional in his moral absolutism but socially tame; unlike Rochester's sexual energy, his abstract passion can easily be contained within the social code which limits companionship between the sexes to marriage. He is, indeed, unconventional only because he presses the orthodox view that duty must conquer feeling to a parodic extreme; and in this he is a peculiarly pure image of the ideology which victimises Jane, as his affinities with Brocklehurst would suggest. Even so, because Rivers forces Brocklehurst's ideology to a pitch of Romantic intensity, he seems to offer Jane a version of what she finally achieves with Rochester: a way of conforming to convention which at the same time draws you beyond it, gathers you into a fuller, finer self-realisation. The point is that such a resolution is available in India for Rivers, but not for Jane. Rivers the missionary is both martyr and hero; Jane would merely have been a martyr.

In so far as Rivers's twisted heroism mixes hard-headed ambition with a touch of Romance, it has its ambiguous appeal to Jane. His detection of kindred impulses in her is shrewd: she has hardly arrived at Thornfield before she is climbing to the leads and scanning the skyline, longing "for a power of vision which might overpass that limit; which might reach the busy world, towns, regions full of life I had heard of but never seen." But Jane's ambition can be assuaged, as Rivers's cannot be. The populous horizons she scans are soon made incarnate in the well-travelled figure of Rochester, brought within the domestic confines of Thornfield to license an equable balance of settlement and stimulation, the foreign and the familiar. Unlike the lower, more provincially-minded gentry, the class to which Rochester belongs is at once local and cosmopolitan, equally at home in the great house and the great world. It is true that Rochester himself feels at home in neither: Thornfield means mad Bertha, and travelling is merely a desperate way of evading her memory. Yet Rochester as Romantic ideal unites Jane's brooding desire for love and security with her eager extraversion to the busy realm of action, the aura of which still glows around her world-weary master. "Romanticism" in Charlotte's fiction commonly has this dual meaning: it signifies the active, worldly, expansive self, but also the conservative impulse to withdraw protectively into some idealised enclave. If Rochester has the edge over Rivers it is partly because he can meet both demands together; Rivers can satisfy only the first.

Rivers's demands, indeed, pull in precisely the opposite direction to Rochester's. He threatens to uproot you lovelessly from idyllic settlement to an *unpleasantly* foreign world, and to a life with no determinate end but death. Jane is certainly willing at times to trade settlement for independence: much as she finds the soft domesticity of the Rivers girls seductive, she is quick to tell St John that she wants an income of her own. In India, however, she would have the worst of all worlds: homelessness, lovelessness and subjugation. She rejects Rivers not only because his demands violate her identity, but because of his imperious masculinity. In India she would be "at his side always, and always restrained, and always checked—forced to keep the fire of [her] nature continually low, to compel it to burn inwardly and never utter a cry, though the imprisoned flame consume vital after vital." Far from combining the excitingly exotic with the lovably familiar, India for Jane would be a mixture of the alien and the over-close. Charlotte's heroines, as we shall see, habitually welcome male domination as a stimulant to their fiery natures; but Rivers's despotism would be merely oppressive. Jane, then, is willing to accompany him to India if she may go free: "I will give the missionary my energies—it is all he wants—but not myself: that would be only adding the husk and shell to the kernel. For them he has no use: I retain them." Scathingly inverting the husk—kernel image, Jane accepts the social role of missionary only if she can preserve unbetrayed the authentic self which belongs to Rochester; and this is hardly a constructive advance on the schizoid condition she has endured for most of her life. Rivers offers a social function which involves the sacrifice of personal fulfilment; Rochester's offer involves exactly the opposite. Both are inferior propositions to becoming Mrs Rochester, at once a fulfilling personal commitment and an enviable public role.

Like Charlotte's other protagonists, Jane does not regard labour as an end in itself. Will and hard work are important, but they must finally culminate in an achieved repose inimical to Rivers's nature. William Crimsworth of *The Professor* is as resolutely single-minded as Rivers in his pursuit of desirable ends, but he knows when to stop: having made his fortune in Europe he retires to England as a gentleman of leisure. With Rivers, however, there is no end to enterprise, as Diana warns Jane: "Think of the task you undertook—one of incessant fatigue: where fatigue kills even the strong; and you are weak. St John—you know him—would urge you to impossibilities: with him there would be no permission to rest during the hot hours; and unfortunately, I have noticed, whatever he exacts, you force yourself to perform." Rivers's goals are of course spiritual, and Crimsworth's material; but the parallel is surely as significant as the contrast. Rivers is a spiritual bourgeois eager to reap inexhaustible profits, unflaggingly devoted to the purchase of souls. His driving will, rigorous self-discipline and fear of emotional entanglements reveal well enough the analogy between Evangelical and entrepreneur. Indeed, Rivers himself candidly admits the connection, if not exactly in those terms. His evangelical zeal is a sublimation of thwarted worldly impulse:

A year ago I was myself intensely miserable, because I thought I had made a mistake in entering the ministry: its uniform duties wearied me to death. I burnt for the more active life of the world—for the more exciting toils of a literary career—for the destiny of an artist, author, orator; anything, rather than that of a priest: yes, the heart of a politician, of a soldier, of a votary of glory, a lover of renown, a luster after power, beat under my curate's surplice. I considered; my life was so wretched, it must be changed, or I must die. After a season of darkness and struggling, light broke and relief fell: my cramped existence all at once spread out to a plain without bounds—my powers heard a call from heaven to rise, gather their full strength, spread their wings and mount beyond ken. God had an errand for me; to bear which afar, to deliver it well, skill and strength, courage and eloquence, the best qualifications of soldier, statesman and orator were all needed: for these all centre in the good missionary.

The similarity with Jane's own frustrated condition is notable, but so too is the difference. Rivers can gain a taste of mundane glory only by embracing danger, obscurity and premature death; Jane moves in the opposite direction, away from obscurity to a success which is at once secure, emotionally fulfilling and, in the world's eyes, highly desirable. In one sense Rivers is too worldly for Jane, trampling ambitiously over the values of cloistered domestic love; in another sense he is not worldly enough, fanatically prepared to squander his life in a remote society. Like Helen Burns, he signifies a perspective which it is vital to acknowledge but perilous to take literally; and the fact that the novel allows him the last word reflects its uneasiness about the victory to which it brings Jane. Rivers at least, the final paragraphs seem to proclaim, has not temporised between the competing claims of world and spirit, whereas the novel has indeed negotiated such a compromise on behalf of its heroine.

Yet the uneasiness is strictly qualified, not least because of the disparity between the final pious phrase ("Amen; even so come, Lord Jesus!") and the man we knew, whose self-denial was guiltily entwined with thrusting self-assertion. Rivers *has* temporised between world and spirit, even if we are now asked to forget the fact and revere him as an image of saintly self-surrender. Even that reverence, however, has its limits: Rivers is introduced into the novel just as Jane has made a painfully authentic self-sacrifice, in order to dramatise the dangers inherent in that virtue and so pave the way back to Rochester and life. Jane flippantly denies that her return to Rochester involves any sort of martyrdom ("Sacrifice! What do I sacrifice? Famine for food, expectation for content"), and of course she is right; but besides forestalling our own mixed feelings about Jane's fairytale triumph by saying it for us, the comment is meant to alert us to the real deprivations she has endured, and so obviate any sense that she has won her self-fulfilment on the cheap. Jane and Rochester are also martyrs in their own successful way; and in this sense the final unbanishable image of Rivers is less a critique of their conjugal happiness than a symbol of the suffering they underwent to achieve it—the patron saint, as it were, of the marriage. It is convenient to leave Rivers with the last word when the genuine threat he represents has been nullified.

Authentic though Jane's renunciation of Rochester is, it has much in common with Rivers's egoistic self-sacrifice to the missionary cause:

> Feeling . . . clamoured wildly. "Oh, comply!" it said. "Think of his misery; think of his danger—look at his state when left alone. . . . Who in the world cares for *you?* or who will be injured by what you do?"
>
> Still indomitable was the reply—"*I* care for myself. The more solitary, the more friendless, the more unsustained I am, the more I will respect myself. I will keep the law given by God; sanctioned by man."

Jane responds similarly to St John's sneer that she refuses his offer because she is afraid of death. "I am. God did not give me my life to throw away; and to do as you wish me would, I begin to think, be almost equivalent to committing suicide." For someone as socially isolated as Jane, the self is all one has; and it is not to be recklessly invested in dubious enterprises. "Self-possession" comes to assume a meaning deeper than the coolly impenetrable composure it signifies in all Charlotte's novels: it suggests also a nurturing and hoarding of the self, a prudent refusal to yield it prematurely in ways which might lead to rash dissipation rather than to increase and enrichment. It is a sense of the self which springs in part from the condition of orphanage. Like almost all of Charlotte's protagonists, Jane is stripped from the outset of significant ties of kin; the self is less a relational reality than a watchful, alien presence on the periphery of others' lives. "You have no business to take our books," John Reed tells her; "you are a dependant, mamma says; you have no money; your father left you none; you ought to beg, and not to live here with gentlemen's children like us, and eat the same meals we do, and wear clothes at our mamma's expense." For John Reed, who you are is a function of your role within a defined system of kinship; for an orphaned outsider like Jane, identity is at once dependent on and denied by one's relatives. It is this which is at the root of her terror and estrangement, as an "uncongenial alien permanently intruded on [Mrs Reed's] family"; she feels secure only when a stranger enters the room. But if orphanage abandons the self to solitude, it also releases it into freedom. "I am glad you are no relation of mine," Jane cries defiantly to Mrs Reed, and looking at what happens to the Reed family one can see her point. That cloyingly permissive world, cohered in part by the violence it wreaks on the scapegoat alien, leads to dissipation in John, emotional withering in Eliza, witless frivolity in Georgiana and premature death for the harassed mother. The Reed family is a nexus of conflict which Jane is indeed well out of; her later return to Gateshead demonstrates how well she has prospered by independent effort and how little she needs them—how much, in a satisfying inversion of the power-relationship, they now need her. To be bereft of relations is pitiable, but breaking ties proves exhilarating: after her scorching denunciation of Mrs Reed, "my soul began to expand, to exult, with the strangest sense of freedom, of triumph, I ever felt. It seemed as if an invisible bond had burst, and that I had struggled out into unhoped-for liberty." Liberty and alienation are closely linked, as Jane implies when Rochester wonders prophetically whether anyone will meddle with their marriage arrangements: "There is no one to meddle, sir. I have no kindred to interfere." Rochester is less fortunate than Jane in this respect: it is his interfering kinsman who wrecks his plans. Being alone entails the bondage of earning your living unsupported, but unshackles you from inherited duties into relative mobility; if there is nobody to love you there is equally nobody to hold you back. It is an ambiguity illustrated in Jane's response to leaving Lowood: she is uncertain how far severing that bond involves freedom or servitude. Leaving school means venturing into a world whose very threats seem enthralling: "I remembered that the real world was wide, and that a varied field of hopes and fears, of sensations and excitements, awaited those who had courage to go forth into its expanse, to seek real knowledge of life amidst its perils." But the buoyancy of the enterprising individualist with the world at her feet is immediately deflated. Jane's prayers for liberty, and then—rationally paring down her hubristic demands—for at least "change and stimulus," are scattered to the winds; in the end she settles glumly for "at least a new servitude." All the oppressed self can finally affirm is a refreshingly novel kind of passivity.

At the centre of all Charlotte's novels, I am arguing, is a figure who either lacks or deliberately cuts the bonds of kinship. This leaves the self a free, blank, "pre-social" atom: free to be injured and exploited, but free also to progress, move through the class-structure, choose and forge relationships, strenuously utilise its talents in scorn of autocracy or paternalism. The novels are deeply informed by this bourgeois ethic, but there is more to be said than that. For the social status finally achieved by the *déraciné* self is at once meritoriously won and inherently proper. Jane's uncle is said to be a tradesman, and the Reeds despise her for it; but Bessie comments that the Eyres were as much gentry as the Reeds, and her Rivers cousins have an impressively ancient lineage. Rochester seems a grander form of gentry, and Jane's relationship with him is of course socially unequal; but it is, nevertheless, a kind of returning home as well as an enviable move upwards. Given relationships are certainly constrictive: they mediate a suave violence deep-seated in society itself, as John Reed's precociously snobbish remark suggests. But knowing where you genetically belong still counts for a good deal in the end. Charlotte's fiction portrays the unprotected self in its lonely conquest of harsh conditions, and so intimates a meritocratic vision; but individualist self-reliance leads you to roles and relations which are objectively fitting.

Jane, then, disowns what second-hand kin she has, caring never to see the Reeds again, surviving instead by her own talents; she creates the relationships which matter, those of spiritual rather than blood affinity. ("I believe [Rochester] is of mine;—I am sure he is,—I feel akin to him . . . though rank and wealth sever us widely, I have something in my brain and heart, in my blood and nerves, that assimilates me mentally to him." Spiritual affinity, indeed, is more physical and full-blooded than the icy *rapport* one has with literal kinsfolk like Rivers. In this as in other ways, however, Jane is granted the best of both worlds. Just as her resources for solitary survival run out, on the long exhausting flight from Thornfield, she is supplied with a new set of kinsfolk who turn out this time to be pleasant. The Rivers sisters provide a cultivated retreat into which Jane can temporarily relax; she rests her head on Diana's lap in delighted gratitude at her discovery of blood-relations, even though the event will prove merely a stopping-off place *en route* to the grander gentility of Rochester. This time, however, her relation to kinsfolk is not that of servile dependence. On the contrary, it is they who are now in part dependent on her: each of them gets a quarter share of her newfound wealth. The legacy allows Jane to combine sturdy independence with a material sealing of her affinity with others. Given relationships are good, if you may negotiate them on your own terms; kinsmen are both gift and threat. It is an ambivalence reflected in Jane's feelings towards Mrs Reed: she upbraids her hotly for neglecting familial duty, but curiously excuses that brutality by wondering "how could she really like an interloper not of her race, and unconnected with her, after her husband's death, by any tie?" Whether "race" matters or not seems a moot point in Jane's own mind.

Jane's relative isolation from given relationships results in a proud autonomy of spirit, one which in some ways implicitly questions the class-structure. She has too much self-respect to lavish her love on an unresponsive Rochester: "He is not of your order; keep to your caste; and be too self-respecting to lavish the love of the whole heart, soul, and strength, where such a gift is not wanted and may be despised." Yet the comment, of course, endorses the class-structure as well as suggesting the spiritual inferiority of one's betters: if the callously insensitive aristocrat cannot recognise a gift when he sees one, then it is wise to remain self-righteously on one's own side of the social divide. In so far as it is for him to make the overture, Jane's attitude combines deference with independence; yet "independence" is a thoroughly ambiguous term. It means not wanting to be a servant, which implies a class-judgement on those below you as well as suggesting a radical attitude to those above. Jane's rebellion against the Reeds engages certain egalitarian feelings: she rejects the idea of paternalist benefaction as disagreeable, and later values her equal relationship with Mrs Fairfax for the freedom it brings. "The equality between her and me was real; not the mere result of condescension on her part; so much the better—my position was all the freer." But independence in this society involves attaining a precarious gentility (Bessie has to admit that the adult Jane is now, at least, a lady), and that in turn entails a sharp eye for the nuance of social distinction. Jane is furious with the Reeds because they treat her as a servant when she isn't one; her smouldering hatred of their snobbery is thus shot through with shared class-assumptions about the poor. ("No; I should not like to belong to poor people.") Her response to the pupils at Morton school is similarly double-edged: distasteful though she finds their unmannerliness, she "must not forget that these coarsely-clad little peasants are of flesh and blood as good as the scions of the gentlest genealogy; and that the germs of native excellence, refinement, intelligence, kind feeling, are as likely to exist in their hearts as in those of the best born." The demotic generosity of this is sharply qualified by that stern self-reminder; Jane's doctrine of spiritual equality stems logically from her own experience, but it has to fight hard against the social discriminations bred into an expensively clad child. (Her egalitarian defence of the "British peasantry" is based, ironically, on a dogma of chauvinist superiority: they are at least preferable to their "ignorant, coarse, and besotted" European counterparts.) Jane feels degraded by her role as schoolmistress ("I had taken a step which sank instead of raising me in the scale of social existence"), but guiltily scorns the feeling as "idiotic"; and that tension deftly defines the petty-bourgeois consciousness which clings to real class-distinctions while spiritually rejecting them. She is, for instance, priggishly quick to point out to the Rivers' servant Hannah that she may be a beggar but at least she is a high-class one:

> "Are you book-learned?" [Hannah] inquired, presently.
> "Yes, very."

The snobbish Hannah must be given an object-lesson in social equality, taught not to judge by appearances, so Jane reveals how superior she is to the old woman. Even in beggary class counts: St John Rivers, presumably noting Jane's refined accent when Hannah turns her from his door, surmises instantly that this is a "peculiar case." Jane's insistence on getting past the servant and appealing to the young ladies glimpsed within is, indeed, sound class tactics: the sisters are presented as idealised versions of herself, quiet, spiritual and self-composed.

Jane's relationship with Rochester is marked by these ambiguities of equality, servitude and independence. He himself conceives of the union in terms of spiritual equality: " 'My bride is here,' he said, again drawing me to him, 'because my equal is here, and my likeness. Jane, will you marry me?' " Far from offering a radically alternative ethic, spiritual equality is what actually smooths your progress through the class-system; Rochester may be spiritually egalitarian but he is still socially eligible. Jane is on the whole submissive to social hierarchy but shares her master's view that spiritual qualities count for more: she has no hesitation in dismissing Blanche Ingram as inferior to herself. She wants a degree of independence in marriage—" 'It would indeed be a relief,' I thought, 'if I had ever so small an independency' "—but it is, significantly, "small": she can hope to bring Rochester an accession of fortune but hardly to get on genuinely equal terms. Independence, then, is an intermediate position between complete equality and excessive docility: it allows you freedom, but freedom within a proper deference.

When stung to righteous anger, Jane can certainly claim a fun-

damental human equality with her employer: "Do you think, because I am poor, obscure, plain, and little, I am soulless and heartless?" There are, in fact, reasons other than simple humanitarian ones
why Jane and Rochester are not as socially divided as may at first
appear. Rochester, the younger son of an avaricious landed gentleman, was denied his share in the estate and had to marry instead into
colonial wealth; Jane's colonial uncle dies and leaves her a sizeable
legacy, enough for independence. The colonial trade which signified
a decline in status for Rochester signifies an advance in status for
Jane, so that although they are of course socially unequal, their for-
tunes spring from the same root. Yet Jane does not finally claim
equality with Rochester; the primary terms on which Charlotte
Brontë's fiction handles relationships are those of dominance and
submission. The novels dramatise a society in which almost all human relationships are power-struggles; and because "equality" therefore comes to be defined as equality of power, it is an inevitably
complicated affair. Jane serves in the end "both for [Rochester's] prop
and guide," which is an interestingly ambiguous situation. It suggests subservience, and so perpetuates their previous relationship;
but the subservience is also, of course, a kind of leadership. Whether
she likes it or not, Jane finally comes to have power over Rochester.
Her ultimate relation to him is a complex blend of independence (she
comes to him on her own terms, financially self-sufficient), submis-
siveness and control.

This complex blend is a recurrent feature of relationships in the
novels. Charlotte's protagonists want independence, but they also
desire to dominate; and their desire to dominate is matched only by
their impulse to submit to a superior will. The primary form assumed by this ambiguity is a sexual one: the need to venerate and
revere, but also to exercise power, enacts itself both in a curious
rhythm of sexual roles. The maimed and blinded Rochester, for example, is in an odd way even more "masculine" than he was before
(he is "brown," "shaggy," "metamorphosed into a lion"), but because he is helpless he is also "feminine"; and Jane, who adopts a
traditionally feminine role towards him ("It is time some one undertook to rehumanise you"), is thereby forced into the male role of
protectiveness. She finds him both attractive and ugly, as he finds
her both plain and fascinating. Rochester's lack of conventional good
looks, in contrast to Rivers's blandly classical features, reflects his
idiosyncratic roughness and so underlines his male mastery, but it

also makes him satisfyingly akin to Jane herself. (A sexual ambiguity prefigured in Rochester's masquerading as an old gypsy woman. Then he was a masculine female, now he is a feminine male. The gypsy image occurs early in the novel in the song Bessie sings to Jane, as an image of the unorthodox freedom of those so low in the class-structure as to be effectively "outside" it; it is used similarly of Heathcliff in *Wuthering Heights*. Its association with Rochester seems appropriate: he is both unconventional and "free" of the class-structure in the peculiar sense in which those who control it are.) Blanche Ingram is a "beauty," but her aggressive masculinity contrasts sharply with Jane's pale subduedness; her dominative nature leads her to desire a husband who will be a foil rather than a rival to her, but it also prompts her to despise effeminate men and admire strong ones:

> "I grant an ugly *woman* is a blot on the fair face of creation; but as to the *gentlemen,* let them be solicitous to possess only strength and valour: let their motto be:—Hunt, shoot and fight: the rest is not worth a fillip. Such should be my device, were I a man."
>
> "Whenever I marry," she continued, after a pause which none interrupted, "I am resolved my husband shall not be a rival, but a foil to me. I will suffer no competitor near the throne; I shall exact an undivided homage; his devotions shall not be shared between me and the shape he sees in his mirror."

The arrogance of this, of course, counts heavily against Blanche; it is hardly likely to charm the listening Rochester. Jane, who shares Blanche's liking for "devilish" men, knows better than she does how they are to be handled—when to exert her piquant will and when to be cajolingly submissive:

> I knew the pleasure of vexing and soothing him by turns; it was one I chiefly delighted in, and a sure instinct always prevented me from going too far: beyond the verge of provocation I never ventured; on the extreme brink I liked well to try my skill. Retaining every minute form of respect, every propriety of my station, I could still meet him in argument without fear or uneasy restraint: this suited both him and me.

Jane moves deftly between male and female roles in her courtship of Rochester; unlike Blanche, who is tall, dark and dominating like Rochester himself, she settles astutely for a vicarious expression of her own competitive maleness through him. She preserves the proprieties while turning them constantly to her advantage, manipulating convention for both self-protection and self-advancement.

This simultaneity of attraction and antagonism, reverence and dominance, is relevant to a more general ambiguity about power which pervades Charlotte's fiction. It parallels and embodies the conflicting desires of the oppressed outcast for independence, for passive conformity to a secure social order, and for avenging self-assertion over that order. Revenge does not, in fact, seem too strong a word for what happens at the end of *Jane Eyre.* Jane's repressed indignation at a dominative society, prudently swallowed back throughout the book, is finally released—not by Jane herself, but by the novelist; and the victim is the symbol of that social order, Rochester. The crippled Rochester is the novel's sacrificial offering to social convention, to Jane's subconscious hostility and, indeed, to her own puritan guilt; by satisfying all three demands simultaneously, it allows her to adopt a suitably subjugated role while experiencing a fulfilling love and a taste of power. Jane's guilt about Rochester's passion and her own is strikingly imaged in the grotesque figure of Bertha: the Bertha who tries on Jane's wedding veil is a projection of Jane's sexually tormented subconsciousness, but since Bertha is masculine, black-visaged and almost the same height as her husband, she appears also as a repulsive symbol of Rochester's sexual drive. The point of the novel's conclusion is to domesticate that drive so that it ceases to be minatory while remaining attractive. In the end, the outcast bourgeoise achieves more than a humble place at the fireside: she also gains independence vis-à-vis the upper class, and the right to engage in the process of taming it. The worldly Rochester has already been purified by fire; it is now for Jane to rehumanise him. By the device of an ending, bourgeois initiative and genteel settlement, sober rationality and Romantic passion, spiritual equality and social distinction, the actively affirmative and the patiently deferential self, can be merged into mythical unity.

The End of *Jane Eyre* and the Creation of a Feminist Myth

Helene Moglen

In deciding to leave Rochester, Jane takes the first crucial step toward independence. She has discovered that there is, after all, something more important to her than pleasing those whom she loves, or giving satisfaction to those who love her. Despite the pain of her conflict, she has acted decisively to preserve her own integrity. At the moment of her decision, Jane returns to the critical scene of her childhood. She is alone in her room as she was alone then—powerless before external circumstances and internal pressures. The limits of the rational world are lost in the boundless universe of imagination:

> That night I never thought to sleep: but a slumber fell on me as soon as I lay down in bed. I was transported in thought to the scenes of childhood: I dreamt I lay in the red-room at Gateshead; that the night was dark, and my mind impressed with strange fears. The light that long ago had struck me into syncope, recalled in this vision, seemed glidingly to mount the wall, and tremblingly to pause in the centre of the obscured ceiling. I lifted up my head to look: the roof resolved to clouds, high and dim; the gleam was such as the moon imparts to vapours she is about to sever. I watched her come—watched with the strangest anticipation; as though some word of doom were to be

From *Charlotte Brontë: The Self Conceived.* © 1976 by Helene Moglen. Norton, 1976.

written on her disk. She broke forth as never moon yet
burst from cloud: a hand first penetrated the sable folds
and waved them away; then, not a moon, but a white human form shown in the azure, inclining a glorious brow
earthward. It gazed and gazed on me. It spoke, to my
spirit: immeasureably distant was the tone, yet so near, it
whispered in my heart—
    "My daughter, flee temptation!"
    "Mother, I will."

The terrifying supernatural experience of the red-room is confronted
and resolved at last. The strange powers of the nonhuman world
seem now but sympathetic extensions of the compelling, equally
mysterious forces of the personality. The authority which Jane has
sought is female: the moon, maternal nature, the mother within herself—a cosmic and personal principle of order and control.

The trauma at Gateshead had first been neutralized in the experience at Lowood and now, as part of the more profound conflict of
Thornfield, is finally resolved. But the antithetical claims which
emerged from Jane's relationship with Rochester have still to be reconciled: the needs of the self and the demands of the "other": passion
and discipline, egotism and denial. The dialectic proceeds. The first
antithesis to Jane's emotionality had been represented by Helen
Burns. The second is offered in the more developed and sophisticated form of St. John Rivers. The allegorical movement of self-
discovery, present throughout the novel, is intensified here and its
Christian structure is emphasized as Jane moves once again into a
level of experience that is social and moral rather than personally and
sexually defined.

At Lowood Jane was drawn out of the private fantasy world into
which she had been thrust by deprivation. Now, after rejecting the
romantic idolatry which parallels her childhood experience on another level, she must consciously relocate herself in a complex hierarchy of values: redefining her relationship to God, to nature, to a
heterogeneous society previously unknown. She must create a personality independent enough to be separate within the unity of love,
secure enough sexually to temper the passion that cloaks self-
abnegation. Hers is a radical trial and is expressed through Christian
parable.

Fleeing temptation, Jane is set down at Whitcross which "is no town, nor even a hamlet; it is but a stone pillar set up where four roads meet." She is at a beginning and must discover her own way. Like Bunyan's pilgrim, Christian, she is bereft of friends and family: homeless and penniless. She must be purged of all human vanity, enduring the humiliation of body and spirit. At first she finds comfort in the maternal nature which had always before offered her solace:

> Nature seemed to me benign and good: I thought she loved me, outcast that I was; and I, who from man could anticipate only mistrust, rejection, insult, clung to her with filial fondness. To-night, at least, I would be her guest—as I was her child: my mother would lodge me without money and without price.

But although she, like all men and women, is related to the natural world, she is not truly a part of it:

> What a golden desert this spreading moor! Everywhere sunshine. I wished I could live in it and on it. I saw a lizard run over the crag; I saw a bee busy among the sweet bilberries. I would fain at the moment have become bee or lizard, that I might have found fitting nutriment, permanent shelter here. But I was a human being, and had a human being's wants: I must not linger where there was nothing to supply them.

God, the Father, had given and secured her life. The only mother she can look to in her present trouble is the mother within. She had discovered her presence on the evening of the departure from Thornfield. Now she must test her power:

> Life, however, was yet in my possession; with all its requirements, and pains, and responsibilities. The burden must be carried; the want provided for; the suffering endured: the responsibility fulfilled. I set out.

At Lowood, hunger seemed in part to be experienced as a need for love. Now the mature Jane confronts similar but more pressing deprivations—starvation and death from exposure. Both are spiritual as well as physical trials. She must again discover and assert the self that can endure. Despite privation (reduced to eating pig's food, brought to a state of beggary) Jane is able to retain a degree of pride appropriate to a character strengthened by the resolve of independent choice and action. And that pride is also softened by new sympathy for those who must, as she, endure the humbling miseries of existence.

Finally, at the point of death, Jane follows a light which leads her to Marsh End, a sanctuary of civilization poised at the edge of the wild, open moors. Looking through the window into the scrupulously clean and pleasant kitchen, she sees an elderly female servant and "two young, graceful women—ladies in every point," one with a dog's head resting on her knee, one with a kitten curled in her lap. Busily involved in their translation of German, they are indeed images of "delicacy and cultivation." (Marsh End seems to be an idealized version of Haworth: Diana Rivers modeled on Emily Brontë; Mary on Anne; their servant, Hannah, on Tabby.) First denied entrance by the servant, Hannah, Jane is finally admitted by St. John Rivers, the brother of Diana and Mary. Her ordeal is ended. She sleeps for three days and three nights, waking only to eat and drink of the food and water of life. Her sleep renews her spirit as it restores her body and is reminiscent of the crisis that followed her ordeal in the red-room. Her first act after awakening is her forgiveness of Hannah for denying her shelter. She cautions this impotent surrogate for the wicked parent that "Some of the best people that ever lived have been as destitute as I am; and if you are a Christian, you ought not to consider poverty a crime." Her clasping of Hannah's hand marks her entrance into the Christian community and her acceptance of social interrelatedness.

Jane had before found comfort and definition in the female environment at Lowood. Now, after completely identifying with Rochester, it is crucial for her to discover herself anew in the images of women. Through her friendship with Diana and Mary Rivers, she becomes stronger, more confident, more focused. In them, free as they are of dependence upon men, strong in their devotion to one another, she finds the form of a new promise of fulfillment. She shares with them their love of nature. She admires and respects their superior learning, their fine minds. She listens to them talk as she had once listened to Maria Temple and Helen Burns, as Charlotte had listened to Emily and Anne. She responds to the authority in Diana—with her it is natural to be passive, "feminine," "to bend where my conscience and self-respect permitted, to an active will." But there is still equality among them. No longer functioning within the authoritarian context of the master-student relationship she had with Rochester, she finds instead that there can be intellectual reciprocity: a sharing of knowledge and gifts, delight in the interaction of personalities. The strength and confidence which she derives from their friendship allow her to accept the job which St. John offers her as teacher in the village school. Assuming this role, she begins to overcome her feelings of social humiliation:

> I felt desolate to a degree. I felt—yes, idiot that I am—I felt degraded. I doubted I had taken a step which sank instead of raising me in the scale of social existence. I was weakly dismayed at the ignorance, the poverty, the coarseness of all I heard and saw round me. But let me not hate and despise myself too much for these feelings: I know them to be wrong—that is a great step gained; I shall strive to overcome them.

And she does largely overcome them (although Jane Eyre, as Charlotte Brontë herself, could not be accused of excessive egalitarian tendencies). She discovers in many of her poor and unlearned students a degree of "natural politeness" and "innate self-respect" which wins her good will and admiration. She takes pride in her accomplishment, in her ability to teach and befriend her students, to be self-sufficient and useful. And her success earns her a position in the little community so that it is enjoyable for her "to live amidst general regard, though it be but the regard of working-people."

The tone of *noblesse oblige* which informs these words provides us with some understanding of the direction which Charlotte Brontë's myth must take. Feminist it might well be, but it is not a feminism which can preach or envision radical social change. Jane, in leaving Rochester, must, it is true, discover her own capacities and strengths. She must learn the pleasures of independence and self-sufficiency. But only economic independence and social position will give her the status essential to the recognition which is the better part of equality.

When St. John informs her of her sizable inheritance and of the fact that he and his sisters are her real cousins, Jane realizes immediately the way in which her life will now be changed. "It was a grand boon doubtless; and independence would be glorious—yes, I felt that—*that* thought swelled my heart." She recognizes also that by sharing her wealth with Diana and Mary she can free them as she herself is now freed, from the dreary servitude of work. She will have with them "a home and connections" and she will be liberated from the necessity of marrying where there is no love.

Discovering her kinship with the Riverses, Jane does, of course follow in the tradition of the heroes and heroines of quest-romance. Social recognition validates internal worth. The implication is that class membership is its very condition. A "lady" is born, not made, even though the secret of her birth might remain hidden. The Riverses are the last of the series of families to which Jane has found herself intimately or distantly connected. In structure they resemble the Reeds and the Ingrams. (The Brocklehurst family can be included here as well. The only difference is that both the Rev. Brocklehurst and his wife are still alive.) All have two daughters (Jane stands outside as a stepsister) and a son. The fathers are dead, the mothers living (Hannah is a kindly, unthreatening, surrogate-mother for the Rivers children as Tabby was for the Brontës). But all the earlier families are "bad" or "false." As indications of the incompleteness of Jane's development, they have signaled successive stages of her "trial": a continuing inability to confront a self that has been "earned." It is with her "real" family that Jane shares her birthright, joyously seizing "the delicious pleasure of which I have caught a glimpse—that of repaying, in part, a mighty obligation, and winning to myself lifelong friends." Here is the multilayered magic of fairy tale. Jane is transformed from stepsister to benefactress. This is the role which Charlotte was to play with her sisters; which she would have wished to play with Branwell, had he been less threatening.

Significantly, it is St. John who pushes her to further recognition of possibility; to further discoveries of herself. He must be the agent of her liberation. If Rochester represents one aspect of Jane's personality, St. John represents the other. On one level, it is the conflict between Byron and the duke of Wellington articulated with psychological subtlety. St. John Rivers is an older and, more importantly, a masculine version of Helen Burns. Without innocence, or naiveté, he is purposeful, directed, threatening. In both of them the spiritual impulse is carried to an extreme: a form of sublimation which can be liberating and creative, but can also destroy.

St. John's Grecian appearance identifies him with the classical virtues of reason and control so admired in *Rasselas*. He is fair and pale, his light is repressed and "burns" as Helen's did, within. While the fire of the red-room and the fire of the wild, impassioned Bertha threaten destruction to others, St. John's fire is, as Jane sees, self-consuming.

> That heart is already laid on a sacred altar: the fire is arranged round it. It will soon be no more than a sacrifice consumed.

In him, Charlotte Brontë has drawn a stunning portrait of the martyr—unsoftened by the childish idealism or female vulnerability which made Helen sympathetic. Defining self-denial as its own virtue, St. John wishes to sacrifice his life to others although he is, by his own admission, a "cold, hard man."

He subscribes, as Helen did, to a Calvinism that is bitter and stern, full of the promise of guilt and punishment. But he identifies himself with the punishing authority of that religion, casting himself as avenging angel rather than as victim. He has found in the missionary's calling a way of channeling his ambitions as soldier, statesman, orator: "a lover of renown, a luster after power," and he brings to his "profession" the hardness and despotism that befit a man of the world. His sadistic arrogance is the male version of Helen's masochism.

Charlotte Brontë describes St. John as "a cold, cumbrous, column." She had used a similar image for Brocklehurst who was "a black pillar . . . a straight, narrow, sable-clad shape." The identification of male sexuality and power on one hand and that same sexuality with rigidity—even death—on the other, is hardly accidental. (It would seem that Brontë was ambivalent about many of the parallels which she suggests between St. John and Brocklehurst. Despite strongly negative aspects of St. John's characterization, Brontë chooses to praise him as a martyr whose way, while flawed and not Jane's own, is still worthy of respect.) The extent to which St. John purchases his religious calling at the cost of sexual passion is illustrated in his abortive relationship with Rosamond Oliver; the charming girl whom he rejects precisely because he is attracted to her. And the extent to which his religious fervor is the result of sexual fear and repression is revealed in his more subtle and complex relationship with Jane.

He is attracted to Jane initially because of her courage in adversity. Knowing her past, he is familiar with the strength of her moral fiber. In her attention to her students he sees that she is diligent, orderly, and energetic as well as intelligent. He recognizes in her desire to share her inheritance, a gift for sacrifice, and he feels in her response to him an appropriate recognition of his power. For these reasons, he concludes that she would make him a useful helpmate. But there is an enormous contradiction in his attitude toward her. He does not want to see her as a woman. He would, in fact, have her deny her sexual nature, her feelings, her body—subordinate that which is most vital in her self to his own spiritual quest. Her passivity and masochism respond to him:

> As for me, I daily wished more to please him: but to do so, I felt daily more and more that I must disown half my nature, stifle my faculties, wrest my tastes from their original bent, force myself to the adoption of pursuits for which I had no natural vocation. He wanted to train me to an elevation I could never reach: it racked me hourly to aspire to the standard he uplifted.

The great problem arises from his insistence that she must join him in his missionary labors, not as a friend, not as a "sister," but as a wife: "A sister might any day be taken from me. I want a wife: a soul helpmeet I can influence efficiently in life and retain absolutely till death." He wants to control her completely. For Jane the temptation is strong. Commitment to the work, even to the death which she sees as the inevitable outcome of her existence: this would focus her life and obscure her love for Rochester by employing her physical and intellectual energies. She is willing to defy society and sacrifice her life to participate in that larger mission in which she can only partially believe. It is possible to compromise worldly interests and spiritual doubts, but she cannot sacrifice her sexuality. And there is no question that her sexuality is at issue.

St. John's manipulative power, the loftiness of his aspirations, the largeness of his will—all evoke a response based upon her habitual tendency to submit to a dominating spirit, her need for approval and respect.

> By degrees he acquired a certain influence over me that took away my liberty of mind: his praise and notice were more restraining than his indifference.

The attraction Jane feels is not unrelated to the idolatry of her love for Rochester. It is that aspect of sexuality which is power-oriented, potentially sadomasochistic:

> Though I have only sisterly affection for him now, yet, if
> forced to be his wife, I can imagine the possibility of con-
> ceiving an inevitable, strange, torturing kind of love for
> him: because he is so talented; and there is often a certain
> heroic grandeur in his look, manner and conversation.

Jane recognizes that St. John would buy her body with the coin of
spirituality, hypocritically posing as God's agent. "Do you think
God will be satisfied with half an oblation?" he asks her. "Will he
accept a mutilated sacrifice? It is the cause of God I advocate: it is
under His standard I enlist you." St. John must make a religious duty
of sexual need. He explicitly denies his own and therefore her sexuality, fearing the passion which would make him mortal and vulnerable. As she comes to understand St. John, Jane is so distressed
by his twisted, sadistic (albeit unconscious) misrepresentation of his
own feeling and by his misunderstanding of hers that she angrily and
openly opposes him. When he says: "Undoubtedly enough of love
would follow upon marriage to render the union right even in your
eyes," she replies: "I scorn your idea of love . . . I scorn the counter-
feit sentiment you offer: yes, St. John, and I scorn you when you
offer it." It is the extraordinary contempt of a virginal young woman
for the Victorian concept of sex as duty, for the Victorian denial of
the dignity of human passion. But there still remains in Jane the
other side of that Victorian repression: the overwhelming desire to
submit to a power that will envelope her, possess her, negate her.

> I was tempted to cease struggling with him—to rush
> down the torrent of his will into the gulf of his existence,
> and there lose my own.

Well might she say, "I was almost as hard beset by him now as I had
been once before, in a different way, by another."

In the final scene between Jane and St. John, the language of
spiritual transfiguration is interlaced with the language and imagery
of sexuality. The images of the red-room are recalled as well as the
dreams that preceded Jane's decision at Thornfield:

> I stood motionless under my hierophant's touch. My re-
> fusals were forgotten—my fears overcome—my wres-
> tlings paralyzed. The Impossible—i.e. my marriage with
> St. John—was fast becoming the Possible. All was chang-
> ing utterly, with a sudden sweep. Religion called—Angels
> beckoned—God commanded—life rolled together like a

scroll—death's gates opening, shewed eternity beyond: it seemed, that for safety and bliss there, all here might be sacrificed in a second. The dim room was full of visions.

The one candle was dying out: the room was full of moonlight. My heart beat fast and thick: I heard its throb. Suddenly it stood still to an inexpressible feeling that thrilled it through, and passed at once to my head and extremities. The feeling was not like an electric shock; but it was quite as sharp, as strange, as startling: it acted on my senses as if their utmost activity hitherto had been but torpor; from which they were now summoned, and forced to wake.

Two other profound psychic experiences had occasioned the fear of loss and violation sufficiently terrifying to induce unconsciousness. This third time, much strengthened, Jane is impelled to self-assertive action. Now she is released by orgasmic convulsion into spiritual resolution and sexual redefinition. The response is summoned by the sexual component of St. John's power, but it yields awareness and self-discovery instead of dread annihilation. Much of the dangerous appeal of Rochester's sexuality had derived from a similar charisma of power (a charisma not completely lacking, as masculine force, even in Brocklehurst and John Reed). That appeal is experienced here fully—and finally, absolutely rejected. (Not least of all, the brother-lover is implicitly rejected, literally "sacrificed," as we later learn, in favor of the lover-husband.) Now Jane is free to explore the potential that remains. When she hears Rochester's voice calling to her, she responds as surely to the need it expresses as she responds to the need in herself which she must acknowledge. Rather than accepting the sublimation of desire in a patriarchal religious value system, she finds spiritual meaning in human experience. She rejects sexual passion that derives its force from masochistic self-denial and insists that duty and obligation must be placed within the context of a generous and reciprocal human love.

In rejecting St. John, Jane comes to terms with her need for an external authority. She completes the move toward independence begun in the red-room and continued in her departure from Thornfield. In rejecting St. John's repressive sexuality she rejects the perverse sadomasochism it implies, and she attempts to distinguish the sexuality of love from the sexuality of power: the love born of equality from the love subject to idolatry.

This is the last of the symbolic "separations." At every previous point of parting (from Bessie, Helen, Maria Temple, Rochester) Jane's "self," apparently severed and divided, has become stronger and more integrated than before. The separation from St. John marks the ultimate resolution of her spiritual and sexual being, but the transformation of the Edward Rochester to whom she returns is the crucial condition of the actualization of that being and therefore of the viability of the new Romantic myth which the novel has articulated.

In her return to Thornfield, Jane is as little motivated by moral considerations as she had been before in her departure. She is driven by premonition and passion rather than principle or judgment.

> Could I but see him! Surely, in that case, I should not be
> so mad as to run to him? I cannot tell—I am not certain.
> And if I did—what then? God bless him! What then? Who
> would be hurt by my once more tasting the life his glance
> can give me?

She finds Thornfield in ruins: destroyed by the mystery of fire and blood which had been secreted within it for so long: set aflame by Bertha, who was killed while attempting to escape from her husband. The house is the very image of its former master who, Samson-like, maddened by loneliness, desperate and trapped within the futility of his rebellion, had pulled his home down about himself, blinded and crippled his body, deprived himself of that which he had most valued and most feared: the power and pride of his "masculinity." The ambivalence of the Byronic hero towards his own sexuality is nowhere better expressed than in Rochester's attempted rescue of his mad wife, described to Jane by one of the townspeople:

> I witnessed, and several more witnessed Mr. Rochester as-
> cend through the skylight to the roof; we heard him call
> "Bertha!" We saw him approach her; and then, ma'am, she
> yelled, and gave a spring, and the next minute she lay
> smashed on the pavement.

The saviour appears to the victim as avenger and rescue itself becomes a kind of murder. Rochester's heroism, not unlike Byron's own, is realized in self-destruction.

Jane seeking Rochester at Ferndean reminds us paradoxically— yet justly—of the Prince who comes to awaken the sleeping Beauty with a kiss. Their roles are now reversed. All is dark and overgrown, the decaying house buried in the gloomy, tangled forest as Rochester's spirit is hidden in his broken body. Watching him emerge, Jane thinks "of some wronged and fettered wild-beast or bird, dangerous to approach in his sullen woe . . . the caged eagle, whose gold-ringed eyes cruelty has extinguished." That she had in past times reminded him of a small, helpless bird trapped in a nest metaphorizes our sense of their role reversal.

Brontë has afflicted her hero with the Christian punishment appropriate to one who has "committed adultery in his heart" and "put aside his wife." It is the punishment prophesied earlier by Jane in the first agony of her discovery of Rochester's wife.

> You shall, yourself, pluck out your right eye; yourself cut off your right hand: your heart shall be the victim; and you, the priest, to transfix it. [See Matt. 5:27–32. Rochester's left eye remains blind. We are told on p. 552 (of Jane Jack and Margaret Smith's Oxford edition) that he loses his left hand, but on p. 557, Jane contradicts herself and says it was his right hand that was destroyed.]

And the punishment is appropriate in far more subtle ways as well: in ways which speak to the social, psychological, and sexual disease of which "romantic love" is a symptom. In the cost to Rochester of the resolution of Jane's conflict, the severity of social and psychological pressures are most painfully demonstrated. Just as Henry Hastings's disintegration was essential to Elizabeth's discovery of her own abilities and as Charlotte's personal and artistic growth were predicated upon both Branwell's moral and physical collapse and Patrick Brontë's increasing dependence, so too can Jane's development be maintained only at the cost of Rochester's romantic self-image. Rochester's mutilation is, in the terms of this nascent feminist myth, the necessary counterpart of Jane's independence: the terrible condition of a relationship of equality.

But what, in fact, is the nature of this "equality?" Jane's flight from the orgasmic knowledge of St. John's sexual power and Rochester's last catastrophic struggle with his vampire-bride are not the bases of a mature sexuality which is an extension of social liberation. They are rather preludes to the desexualization which is the unhappy compromise necessary when psychosexual need is unsupported by social reality or political self-consciousness. The mystery of fire and blood is not solved. It is simply eradicated. Jane's sense of Rochester, as she looks at him on the morning after her return, is crucial:

> His countenance reminded one of a lamp quenched, waiting to be relit—and alas! it was not himself that could kindle the lustre of animated expression: he was dependent on another for that office.

He is devitalized; the fire of his passion burnt to ash; the quick of his nature paralyzed. He is not the bereaved lover, expectantly awaiting his mistress's return. His is a comatose soul, unable to cry out for rebirth. It is not a lover he requires, but a mother who can offer him again the gift of life. And it is this function which Jane will gratefully assume.

> I love you better now, when I can really be useful to you, than I did in your state of proud independence, when you disdained every part but that of the giver and protector.

Brontë, dividing her time between the writing of her novel and the nursing of her weak and sightless father, could well have spoken these words with Jane. They belong to the virginal daughter who has been magically transformed—without the mediation of sexual contact—into the noble figure of the nurturing mother. Once the magical transformation has taken place, the dependence defined, the partial restoration of Rochester's vision cannot reverse the pattern of relationship any more easily than the removal of Patrick Brontë's cataracts could completely reestablish the old patriarchal order.

Jane's money and social status, even her confidence and self-knowledge, would not have offered her sufficient protection against the psychosexual power of Rochester, her "master"; would not have defended her against the arrogance and pride supported by society through its laws, its structures, its attitudes, its mythology. Nor would her new position, her developed self, have protected Rochester from the fears and actual dangers associated with the "masculine" role assigned to him. So strong are these external forces that the reduction of Rochester's virility and the removal of them both from contact with society are necessary to maintain the integrity of the emergent female self. Rochester is brought into the "female" world of love and morality, out of the "masculine" universe of power: out of society, into Jane's sphere of psychic functioning. His transformation heralds the death of the Byronic hero whose many charms

were the imaginative instruments of a sexually repressive and oppressive society. But the society into which his maimed Victorian
spirit is reborn is still more repressive and more closed. Brontë's
myth reflects those social limitations even as it attempts to define a
new feminist freedom. Rochester is, in this sense, a pivotal figure;
marking the transition from the Romantic to the modern hero, her-
alding the paralyzing alienation which will be chronicled by Dickens, by Thackeray, by George Eliot, and Lawrence: by Melville, by
Mann, by Kafka, and Dostoyevski. His mangled body projects his
psychic scars. His absence of vitality derives from a psychic illness
which will become, in many of his successors, spiritual death.

Rochester is the representative and victim of forces over which
Jane has triumphed in order to redefine herself. But the self which
emerges from the sequential struggles it endures cannot be tested
again by former adversaries. The allegorical quest follows a necessary and irreversible path. In its victories, the ego absorbs those
components of reality which it has successfully confronted, negating
their existence as objective form. The aggressive, even sadistic "masculinity" of John Reed, and Brocklehurst, of St. John and the
younger Rochester are all contained within the humbled and broken
hero whom Jane ultimately nourishes and sustains. This is, of
course, the fantasy element of Brontë's feminist myth. It would not
be for almost fifty years that social change and aroused political consciousness would make it possible to test an awareness and achievement like Jane Eyre's against realistic pressures. In England it would
not be until the twentieth century and the fiction of D. H. Lawrence
that the descendants of the maimed Rochester and the liberated Jane
would be able to face each other in the full complexity of their social,
sexual, and psychological conflicts. (One thinks, for example, of
Gerald and Gudrun in *Women in Love,* of Ursula and Skrebensky in
The Rainbow, and Clifford and Constance in *Lady Chatterley's Lover.*
It ought to be noted that Lawrence's perspective was hardly feminist.) In our own time we struggle still to break through the irrational identification of phallic potency with political, social, and economic domination.

There is, in the naive resolution of *Jane Eyre,* an idealization of
Jane and Rochester's life together which is part of the logic of the
psychosexual romance. The last chapter begins with an extraordinary statement that places Jane at the center of the relationship.
"Reader, I married him," she says and continues:

I have now been married ten years. I know what it is to live entirely for and with what I love best on earth. I hold myself supremely blest—blest beyond what language can express; because I am my husband's life as fully as he is mine. No woman was ever nearer to her mate than I am: absolutely more bone of his bone, and flesh of his flesh. I know no weariness of my Edward's society: he knows none of mine, any more than we do of the pulsation of the heart that beats in our separate bosoms; consequently, we are ever together. To be together is for us to be at once as free as in solitude, as gay as in company. We talk, I believe, all day long: to talk to each other is but an animated and audible thinking. All my confidence is bestowed on him; all his confidence is devoted to me: we are precisely suited in character; perfect concord is the result.

But the truth of this relationship is an interior truth, as remote from social reality as are Gateshead, Lowood, Thornfield, Marsh End, and Ferndean—themselves all landscapes of psychological development. It is the truth of Charlotte Brontë's dream that we have here: the truth of her fantasy. To the extent that it dramatizes the conflict of larger social and psychological forces, it offers also the larger truth of myth. But what is extraordinary is that this novel, born of repression and frustration, of limited experience and less hope, should have offered an insight into psychosexual relationships that was visionary in its own time and remains active in ours.

A Dialogue of Self and Soul: Plain Jane's Progress

Sandra M. Gilbert and Susan Gubar

> *I dreamt that I was looking in a glass when a horrible face—the face of an animal—suddenly showed over my shoulder. I cannot be sure if this was a dream, or if it happened.*
> —Virginia Woolf

> *Never mind. . . . One day, quite suddenly, when you're not expecting it, I'll take a hammer from the folds of my dark cloak and crack your little skull like an egg-shell. Crack it will go, the egg-shell; out they will stream, the blood, the brains. One day, one day. . . . One day the fierce wolf that walks by my side will spring on you and rip your abominable guts out. One day, one day. . . . Now, now, gently, quietly, quietly. . . .*
> —Jean Rhys

> *I told my Soul to sing—*
>
> *She said her Strings were snapt—*
> *Her bow—to Atoms blown—*
> *And so to mend her—gave me work*
> *Until another Morn—*
> —Emily Dickinson

If *The Professor* is a somewhat blurred trance-statement of themes and conflicts that dominated Charlotte Brontë's thought far more than she herself may have realized, *Jane Eyre* is a work permeated by angry, *Angrian* fantasies of escape-into-wholeness. Borrowing the mythic quest-plot—but not the devout substance—of Bunyan's male

---

From *The Madwoman in the Attic: The Woman Writer and the Nineteenth-Century Literary Imagination.* © 1979 by Yale University. Yale University Press, 1979.

Pilgrim's Progress, the young novelist seems here definitively to have opened her eyes to female realities within her and around her: confinement, orphanhood, starvation, rage even to madness. Where the fiery image of Lucia, that energetic woman who probably "once wore chains and broke them," is miniaturized in *The Professor,* in *Jane Eyre* (1847) this figure becomes almost larger than life, the emblem of a passionate, barely disguised rebelliousness.

Victorian critics, no doubt instinctively perceiving the subliminal intensity of Brontë's passion, seem to have understood this point very well. Her "mind contains nothing but hunger, rebellion, and rage," Matthew Arnold wrote of Charlotte Brontë in 1853. He was referring to *Villette,* which he elsewhere described as a "hideous, undelightful, convulsed, constricted novel," but he might as well have been speaking of *Jane Eyre,* for his response to Brontë was typical of the outrage generated in some quarters by her first published novel. "Jane Eyre is throughout the personification of an unregenerate and undisciplined spirit," wrote Elizabeth Rigby in *The Quarterly Review* in 1848, and her "autobiography . . . is preeminently an anti-Christian composition. . . . The tone of mind and thought which has fostered Chartism and rebellion is the same which has also written *Jane Eyre.*" Anne Mozley, in 1853, recalled for *The Christian Remembrancer* that "Currer Bell" had seemed on her first appearance as an author "soured, coarse, and grumbling; an alien . . . from society and amenable to none of its laws." And Mrs. Oliphant related in 1855 that "Ten years ago we professed an orthodox system of novel-making. Our lovers were humble and devoted . . . and the only true love worth having was that . . . chivalrous true love which consecrated all womankind . . . when suddenly, without warning, *Jane Eyre* stole upon the scene, and the most alarming revolution of modern times has followed the invasion of *Jane Eyre.*"

We tend today to think of *Jane Eyre* as moral Gothic, "myth domesticated," *Pamela*'s daughter and *Rebecca*'s aunt, the archetypal scenario for all those mildly thrilling romantic encounters between a scowling Byronic hero (who owns a gloomy mansion) and a trembling heroine (who can't quite figure out the mansion's floor plan). Or, if we're more sophisticated, we give Charlotte Brontë her due, concede her strategic as well as her mythic abilities, study the patterns of her imagery, and count the number of times she addresses the reader. But still we overlook the "alarming revolution"—even Mrs. Oliphant's terminology is suggestive—which "followed the invasion of *Jane Eyre*." "Well, obviously *Jane Eyre* is a feminist tract, an argument for the social betterment of governesses and equal rights for women," Richard Chase somewhat grudgingly admitted in 1948. But like most other modern critics, he believed that the novel's power arose from its mythologizing of Jane's confrontation with masculine sexuality.

Yet, curiously enough, it seems not to have been primarily the coarseness and sexuality of *Jane Eyre* which shocked Victorian reviewers (though they disliked those elements in the book), but, as we have seen, its "anti-Christian" refusal to accept the forms, customs, and standards of society—in short, its rebellious feminism. They were disturbed not so much by the proud Byronic sexual energy of Rochester as by the Byronic pride and passion of Jane herself, not so much by the asocial sexual vibrations between hero and heroine as by the heroine's refusal to submit to her social destiny: "She has inherited in fullest measure the worst sin of our fallen nature—the sin of pride," declared Miss Rigby.

> Jane Eyre is proud, and therefore she is ungrateful, too. It pleased God to make her an orphan, friendless, and penniless—yet she thanks nobody, and least of all Him, for the food and raiment, the friends, companions, and instructors of her helpless youth. . . . On the contrary, she looks upon all that has been done for her not only as her undoubted right, but as falling far short of it.

In other words, what horrified the Victorians was Jane's anger. And perhaps they, rather than more recent critics, were correct in their response to the book. For while the mythologizing of repressed rage may parallel the mythologizing of repressed sexuality, it is far more dangerous to the order of society. The occasional woman who has a weakness for black-browed Byronic heroes can be accommodated in novels and even in some drawing rooms; the woman who yearns to escape entirely from drawing rooms and patriarchal mansions obviously cannot. And Jane Eyre, as Matthew Arnold, Miss Rigby, Mrs. Mozley, and Mrs. Oliphant suspected, was such a woman.

Her story, providing a pattern for countless others, is—far more obviously and dramatically than *The Professor*—a story of enclosure and escape, a distinctively female bildungsroman in which the problems encountered by the protagonist as she struggles from the imprisonment of her childhood toward an almost unthinkable goal of mature freedom are symptomatic of difficulties Everywoman in a patriarchal society must meet and overcome: oppression (at Gateshead), starvation (at Lowood), madness (at Thornfield), and coldness (at Marsh End). Most important, her confrontation, not with Rochester but with Rochester's mad wife Bertha, is the book's central confrontation, an encounter—like Frances Crimsworth's fantasy about Lucia—not with her own sexuality but with her own imprisoned "hunger, rebellion, and rage," a secret dialogue of self and soul on whose outcome, as we shall see, the novel's plot, Rochester's fate, and Jane's coming-of-age all depend.

Unlike many Victorian novels, which begin with elaborate expository paragraphs, *Jane Eyre* begins with a casual, curiously enigmatic remark: "There was no possibility of taking a walk that day." Both the occasion ("that day") and the excursion (or the impossibility of one) are significant: the first is the real beginning of Jane's pilgrim's progress toward maturity; the second is a metaphor for the problems she must solve in order to attain maturity. "I was glad" not to be able to leave the house, the narrator continues: "dreadful to me was the coming home in the raw twilight . . . humbled by the consciousness of my physical inferiority" (chap. 1). As many critics have commented, Charlotte Brontë consistently uses the opposed properties of fire and ice to characterize Jane's experiences, and her technique is immediately evident in these opening passages. For while the world outside Gateshead is almost unbearably wintry, the world within is claustrophobic, fiery, like ten-year-old Jane's own mind. Excluded from the Reed family group in the drawing room because *she* is not a "contented, happy, little child"—excluded, that is, from "normal" society—Jane takes refuge in a scarlet-draped window seat where she alternately stares out at the "drear November day" and reads of polar regions in Bewick's *History of British Birds*. The "death-white realms" of the Arctic fascinate her; she broods upon "the multiplied rigors of extreme cold" as if brooding upon her own dilemma: whether to stay in, behind the oppressively scarlet curtain, or to go out into the cold of a loveless world.

Her decision is made for her. She is found by John Reed, the tyrannical son of the family, who reminds her of her anomalous position in the household, hurls the heavy volume of Bewick at her, and arouses her passionate rage. Like a "rat," a "bad animal," a "mad cat," she compares him to "Nero, Caligula, etc." and is borne away to the red-room, to be imprisoned literally as well as figuratively.

For "the fact is," confesses the grownup narrator ironically, "I was [at that moment] a trifle beside myself; or rather *out* of myself, as the French would say. . . . like any other rebel slave, I felt resolved . . . to go all lengths" (chap. 1).

But if Jane was "out of" herself in her struggle against John Reed, her experience in the red-room, probably the most metaphorically vibrant of all her early experiences, forces her deeply into herself. For the red-room, stately, chilly, swathed in rich crimson, with a great white bed and an easy chair "like a pale throne" looming out of the scarlet darkness, perfectly represents her vision of the society in which she is trapped, an uneasy and elfin dependent. "No jail was ever more secure," she tells us. And no jail, we soon learn, was ever more terrifying either, because this is the room where Mr. Reed, the only "father" Jane has ever had, "breathed his last." It is, in other words, a kind of patriarchal death chamber, and here Mrs. Reed still keeps "divers parchments, her jewel-casket, and a miniature of her dead husband" in a secret drawer in the wardrobe (chap. 2). Is the room haunted, the child wonders. At least, the narrator implies, it is realistically if not Gothically haunting, more so than any chamber in, say, *The Mysteries of Udolpho,* which established a standard for such apartments. For the spirit of a society in which Jane has no clear place sharpens the angles of the furniture, enlarges the shadows, strengthens the locks on the door. And the deathbed of a father who was not really her father emphasizes her isolation and vulnerability.

Panicky, she stares into a "great looking glass," where her own image floats toward her, alien and disturbing. "All looked colder and darker in that visionary hollow than in reality," the adult Jane explains. But a mirror, after all, is also a sort of chamber, a mysterious enclosure in which images of the self are trapped like "divers parchments." So the child Jane, though her older self accuses her of mere superstition, correctly recognizes that she is doubly imprisoned. Frustrated and angry, she meditates on the injustices of her life, and fantasizes "some strange expedient to achieve escape from insupportable oppression—as running away, or, if that could not be effected, never eating or drinking more, and letting myself die" (chap. 2). Escape through flight, or escape through starvation: the alternatives will recur throughout *Jane Eyre* and, indeed, as we have already noted [elsewhere], throughout much other nineteenth- and twentieth-century literature by women. In the red-room, however, little Jane chooses (or is chosen by) a third, even more terrifying, alternative: escape through madness. Seeing a ghostly, wandering light, as of the moon on the ceiling, she notices that "my heart beat thick, my head grew hot; a sound filled my ears, which I deemed the rushing of wings; something seemed near me; I was oppressed, suffocated: endurance broke down." The child screams and sobs in anguish, and then, adds the narrator coolly, "I suppose I had a species of fit," for her next memory is of waking in the nursery "and seeing before me a terrible red glare crossed with thick black bars" (chap. 3), merely the nursery fire of course, but to Jane Eyre the child a terrible reminder of the experience she has just had, and to Jane Eyre the adult narrator an even more dreadful omen of experiences to come.

For the little drama enacted on "that day" which opens *Jane Eyre* is in itself a paradigm of the larger drama that occupies the entire book: Jane's anomalous, orphaned position in society, her enclosure in stultifying roles and houses, and her attempts to escape through flight, starvation, and—in a sense which will be explained—madness. And that Charlotte Brontë quite consciously intended the incident of the red-room to serve as a paradigm for the larger plot of her novel is clear not only from its position in the narrative but also from Jane's own recollection of the experience at crucial moments throughout the book: when she is humiliated by Mr. Brocklehurst at Lowood, for instance, and on the night when she decides to leave Thornfield. In between these moments, moreover, Jane's pilgrimage consists of a series of experiences which are, in one way or another, variations on the central, red-room motif of enclosure and escape.

As we noted earlier, the allusion to pilgriming is deliberate, for like the protagonist of Bunyan's book, Jane Eyre makes a life-journey which is a kind of mythical progress from one significantly named place to another. Her story begins, quite naturally, at *Gateshead,* a starting point where she encounters the uncomfortable givens of her career: a family which is not her real family, a selfish older "brother" who tyrannizes over the household like a substitute patriarch, a foolish and wicked "stepmother," and two unpleasant, selfish "stepsisters." The smallest, weakest, and plainest child in the house, she embarks on her pilgrim's progress as a sullen Cinderella, an angry Ugly Duckling, immorally rebellious against the hierarchy that oppresses her: "I know that had I been a sanguine, brilliant, careless, exacting, handsome, romping child—though equally dependent and friendless—Mrs. Reed would have endured my presence more complacently," she reflects as an adult (chap. 2).

But the child Jane cannot, as she well knows, be "sanguine and brilliant." Cinderella never is; nor is the Ugly Duckling, who, for all her swansdown potential, has no great expectations. "Poor, plain, and little," Jane Eyre—her name is of course suggestive—is invisible as air, the heir to nothing, secretly choking with ire. And Bessie, the kind nursemaid who befriends her, sings her a song that no fairy godmother would ever dream of singing, a song that summarizes the plight of all real Victorian Cinderellas:

> My feet they are sore, and my limbs they are weary,
>   Long is the way, and the mountains are wild;
> Soon will the twilight close moonless and dreary
>   Over the path of the poor orphan child.

A hopeless pilgrimage, Jane's seems, like the sad journey of Wordsworth's Lucy Gray, seen this time from the inside, by the child herself rather than by the sagacious poet to whom years have given a philosophic mind. Though she will later watch the maternal moon rise to guide her, now she imagines herself wandering in a moonless twilight that foreshadows her desperate flight across the moors after leaving Thornfield. And the only hope her friend Bessie can offer is, ironically, an image that recalls the patriarchal terrors of the redroom and hints at patriarchal terrors to come—Lowood, Brocklehurst, St. John Rivers:

> Ev'n should I fall o'er the broken bridge passing,
>   Or stray in the marshes, by false lights beguiled,
> Still will my Father, with promise and blessing
>   Take to His bosom the poor orphan child.

It is no wonder that, confronting such prospects, young Jane finds herself "whispering to myself, over and over again" the words of Bunyan's Christian: "What shall I do?—What shall I do?" (chap. 4).

What she does do, in desperation, is burst her bonds again and again to tell Mrs. Reed what she thinks of her, an extraordinarily self-assertive act of which neither a Victorian child nor a Cinderella was ever supposed to be capable. Interestingly, her first such explosion is intended to remind Mrs. Reed that she, too, is surrounded by patriarchal limits: "What would Uncle Reed say to you if he were alive?" Jane demands, commenting, "It seemed as if my tongue pronounced words without my will consenting to their utterance: something spoke out of me over which I had no control" (chap. 4). And indeed, even imperious Mrs. Reed appears astonished by these words. The explanation, "something spoke out of me," is as frightening as the arrogance, suggesting the dangerous double consciousness—"the rushing of wings, something . . . near me"—that brought on the fit in the red-room. And when, with a real sense that "an invisible bond had burst, and that I had struggled out into unhoped-for liberty," Jane tells Mrs. Reed that "I am glad you are no relation of mine" (chap. 4), the adult narrator remarks that "a ridge of lighted heath, alive, glancing, devouring, would have been a meet emblem of my mind"—as the nursery fire was, flaring behind its black grates, and as the flames consuming Thornfield also will be.

Significantly, the event that inspires little Jane's final fiery words to Mrs. Reed is her first encounter with that merciless and hypocritical patriarch Mr. Brocklehurst, who appears now to conduct her on the next stage of her pilgrimage. As many readers have noticed, this personification of the Victorian superego is—like St. John Rivers, his counterpart in the last third of the book—consistently described in phallic terms: he is "a black pillar" with a "grim face at the top . . . like a carved mask," almost as if he were a funereal and oddly Freudian piece of furniture (chap. 4). But he is also rather like the wolf in "Little Red Riding Hood." "What a face he had. . . . What a great nose! And what a mouth! And what large prominent teeth!" Jane Eyre exclaims, recollecting that terror of the adult male animal which must have wrung the heart of every female child in a period when all men were defined as "beasts."

Simultaneously, then, a pillar of society and a large bad wolf, Mr. Brocklehurst has come with news of hell to remove Jane to *Lowood,* the aptly named school of life where orphan girls are starved and frozen into proper Christian submission. Where else would a beast take a child but into a wood? Where else would a column of frozen spirituality take a homeless orphan but to a sanctuary where there is neither food nor warmth? Yet "with all its privations" Lowood offers Jane a valley of refuge from "the ridge of lighted heath," a chance to learn to govern her anger while learning to become a governess in the company of a few women she admires.

Foremost among those Jane admires are the noble Miss Temple and the pathetic Helen Burns. And again, their names are significant. Angelic Miss Temple, for instance, with her marble pallor, is a shrine of ladylike virtues: magnanimity, cultivation, courtesy—and repression. As if invented by Coventry Patmore or by Mrs. Sarah Ellis, that indefatigable writer of conduct books for Victorian girls, she dispenses food to the hungry, visits the sick, encourages the worthy, and averts her glance from the unworthy. " 'What shall I do to gratify myself—to be admired—or to vary the tenor of my existence' are not the questions which a woman of right feelings asks on first awaking to the avocations of the day," wrote Mrs. Ellis in 1844.

> Much more congenial to the highest attributes of woman's character are inquiries such as these: "How shall I endeavor through this day to turn the time, the health, and the means permitted me to enjoy, to the best account? Is any one sick? I must visit their chamber without delay. . . . Is any one about to set off on a journey? I must see that the early meal is spread. . . . Did I fail in what was kind or considerate to any of the family yesterday? I will meet her this morning with a cordial welcome."

And these questions are obviously the ones Miss Temple asks herself, and answers by her actions.

Yet it is clear enough that she has repressed her own share of madness and rage, that there is a potential monster beneath her angelic exterior, a "sewer" of fury beneath this temple. Though she is, for instance, plainly angered by Mr. Brocklehurst's sanctimonious stinginess, she listens to his sermonizing in ladylike silence. Her face, Jane remembers, "appeared to be assuming . . . the coldness and fixity of [marble]; especially her mouth, closed as if it would have required a sculptor's chisel to open it" (chap. 7). Certainly Miss Temple will never allow "something" to speak through her, no wings will rush in her head, no fantasies of fiery heath disturb her equanimity, but she will feel sympathetic anger.

Perhaps for this reason, repressed as she is, she is closer to a fairy godmother than anyone else Jane has met, closer even to a true mother. By the fire in her pretty room, she feeds her starving pupils tea and emblematic seedcake, nourishing body and soul together despite Mr. Brocklehurst's puritanical dicta. "We feasted," says Jane, "as on nectar and ambrosia." But still, Jane adds, "Miss Temple had always something . . . of state in her mien, of refined propriety in her language, which precluded deviation into the ardent, the excited, the eager: something which chastened the pleasure of those who looked on her and listened to her, by a controlling sense of awe" (chap. 8). Rather awful as well as very awesome, Miss Temple is not just an angel-in-the-house; to the extent that her name defines her, she is even more house than angel, a beautiful set of marble columns designed to balance that bad pillar Mr. Brocklehurst. And dispossessed Jane, who is not only poor, plain, and little, but also fiery and ferocious, correctly guesses that she can no more become such a woman than Cinderella can become her own fairy godmother.

Helen Burns, Miss Temple's other disciple, presents a different but equally impossible ideal to Jane: the ideal—defined by Goethe's Makarie—of self-renunciation, of all-consuming (and consumptive) spirituality. Like Jane "a poor orphan child" ("I have only a father; and he . . . will not miss me" [chap. 9]), Helen longs alternately for her old home in Northumberland, with its "visionary brook," and for the true home which she believes awaits her in heaven. As if echoing the last stanzas of Bessie's song, "God is my father, God is my friend," she tells Jane, whose skepticism disallows such comforts, and "Eternity [is] a mighty home, not a terror and an abyss" (chap. 7). One's duty, Helen declares, is to submit to the injustices of this life, in expectation of the ultimate justice of the next: "it is weak and silly to say you *cannot bear* what it is your fate to be required to bear" (chap. 7).

Helen herself, however, does no more than *bear* her fate. "I make no effort [to be good, in Lowood's terms]," she confesses. "I follow as inclination guides me" (chap. 7). Labeled a "slattern" for failing to keep her drawers in ladylike order, she meditates on Charles I, as if commenting on all inadequate fathers ("what a pity . . . he could see no farther than the prerogatives of the crown") and studies *Rasselas,* perhaps comparing Dr. Johnson's Happy Valley to the unhappy one in which she herself is immured. "One strong proof of my wretchedly defective nature," she explains to the admiring Jane, "is that even [Miss Temple's] expostulations . . . have no influence to cure me of my faults." Despite her contemplative purity, there is evidently a "sewer" of concealed resentment in Helen Burns, just as there is in Miss Temple. And, like Miss Temple's, her name is significant. Burning with spiritual passion, she also burns with anger, leaves her things "in shameful disorder," and dreams of freedom in eternity: "By dying young, I shall escape great sufferings," she explains (chap. 9). Finally, when the "fog-bred pestilence" of typhus decimates Lowood, Helen is carried off by her own fever for liberty, as if her body, like Jane's mind, were "a ridge of lighted heath . . . devouring" the dank valley in which she has been caged.

This is not to say that Miss Temple and Helen Burns do nothing to help Jane come to terms with her fate. Both are in some sense mothers for Jane, as Adrienne Rich has pointed out, comforting her, counseling her, feeding her, embracing her. And from Miss Temple, in particular, the girl learns to achieve "more harmonious thoughts: what seemed better regulated feelings had become the inmates of my mind. I had given in allegiance to duty and order. I appeared a disciplined and subdued character" (chap. 10). Yet because Jane is an Angrian Cinderella, a Byronic heroine, the "inmates" of her mind can no more be regulated by conventional Christian wisdom than Manfred's or Childe Harold's thoughts. Thus, when Miss Temple leaves Lowood, Jane tells us, "I was left in my natural element." Gazing out a window as she had on "that day" which opened her story, she yearns for true liberty: "for liberty I uttered a prayer." Her way of confronting the world is still the Promethean way of fiery rebellion, not Miss Temple's way of ladylike repression, not Helen Burns's way of saintly renunciation. What she has learned from her two mothers is, at least superficially, to compromise. If pure liberty is impossible, she exclaims, "then . . . grant me at least a new servitude" (chap. 10).

It is, of course, her eagerness for a new servitude that brings Jane to the painful experience that is at the center of her pilgrimage, the experience of *Thornfield,* where, biblically, she is to be crowned with thorns, she is to be cast out into a desolate field, and most important, she is to confront the demon of rage who has haunted her since her afternoon in the red-room. Before the appearance of Rochester, however, and the intrusion of Bertha, Jane—and her readers—must explore Thornfield itself. This gloomy mansion is often seen as just another Gothic trapping introduced by Charlotte Brontë to make her novel saleable. Yet not only is Thornfield more realistically drawn than, say, Otranto or Udolpho, it is more metaphorically radiant than most Gothic mansions: it is the house of Jane's life, its floors and walls the architecture of her experience.

Beyond the "long cold gallery" where the portraits of alien unknown ancestors hang the way the specter of Mr. Reed hovered in the red-room, Jane sleeps in a small pretty chamber, harmoniously furnished as Miss Temple's training has supposedly furnished her own mind. Youthfully optimistic, she notices that her "couch had no thorns in it" and trusts that with the help of welcoming Mrs. Fairfax "a fairer era of life was beginning for me, one that was to have its

flowers and pleasures, as well as its thorns and toils" (chap. 11).
Christian, entering the Palace Beautiful, might have hoped as much.

The equivocal pleasantness of Mrs. Fairfax, however, like the
ambiguous architecture of Thornfield itself, suggests at once a way
in which the situation at Thornfield reiterates all the other settings
of Jane's life. For though Jane assumes at first that Mrs. Fairfax is her
employer, she soon learns that the woman is merely a house*keeper,*
the surrogate of an absent master, just as Mrs. Reed was a surrogate
for dead Mr. Reed or immature John Reed, and Miss Temple for
absent Mr. Brocklehurst. Moreover, in her role as an extension of
the mysterious Rochester, sweet-faced Mrs. Fairfax herself becomes
mysteriously chilling. "Too much noise, Grace," she says peremp-
torily, when she and Jane overhear "Grace Poole's" laugh as they tour
the third story. "Remember directions!" (chap. 11).

The third story is the most obviously emblematic quarter of
Thornfield. Here, amid the furniture of the past, down a narrow
passage with "two rows of small black doors, all shut, like a corridor
in some Bluebeard's castle" (chap. 11), Jane first hears the "distinct
formal mirthless laugh" of mad Bertha, Rochester's secret wife and
in a sense her own secret self. And just above this sinister corridor,
leaning against the picturesque battlements and looking out over the
world like Bluebeard's bride's sister Anne, Jane is to long again for
freedom, for "all of incident, life, fire, feeling that I . . . had not in
my actual existence" (chap. 12). These upper regions, in other
words, symbolically miniaturize one crucial aspect of the world in
which she finds herself. Heavily enigmatic, ancestral relics wall her
in; inexplicable locked rooms guard a secret which may have something to do with *her;* distant vistas promise an inaccessible but enviable life.

Even more importantly, Thornfield's attic soon becomes a complex focal point where Jane's own rationality (what she has learned
from Miss Temple) and her irrationality (her "hunger, rebellion and
rage") intersect. She never, for instance, articulates her rational desire
for liberty so well as when she stands on the battlements of Thornfield, looking out over the world. However offensive these thoughts
may have been to Miss Rigby—and both Jane and her creator obviously suspected they would be—the sequence of ideas expressed in
the famous passage beginning "Anybody may blame me who likes"
is as logical as anything in an essay by Wollstonecraft or Mill. What
is somewhat irrational, though, is the restlessness and passion

which, as it were, italicize her little meditation on freedom. "I could not help it," she explains,

> the restlessness was in my nature, it agitated me to pain sometimes. Then my sole relief was to walk along the corridor of the third story, backwards and forwards, safe in the silence and solitude of the spot, and allow my mind's eye to dwell on whatever bright visions rose before it.

And even more irrational is the experience which accompanies Jane's pacing:

> When thus alone, I not unfrequently heard Grace Poole's laugh: the same peal, the same low, slow ha! ha! which, when first heard, had thrilled me: I heard, too, her eccentric murmurs; stranger than her laugh.
>
> (chap. 12)

Eccentric murmurs that uncannily echo the murmurs of *Jane's* imagination, and a low, slow ha! ha! which forms a bitter refrain to the tale *Jane's* imagination creates. Despite Miss Temple's training, the "bad animal" who was first locked up in the red-room is, we sense, still lurking somewhere, behind a dark door, waiting for a chance to get free. That early consciousness of "something near me" has not yet been exorcised. Rather, it has intensified.

Many of Jane's problems, particularly those which find symbolic expression in her experiences in the third story, can be traced to her ambiguous status as a governess at Thornfield. As M. Jeanne Peterson points out, every Victorian governess received strikingly conflicting messages (she was and was not a member of the family, was and was not a servant). Such messages all too often caused her features to wear what one contemporary observer called "a fixed sad look of despair." But Jane's difficulties arise also, as we have seen, from her constitutional *ire;* interestingly, none of the women she meets at Thornfield has anything like that last problem, though all suffer from equivalent ambiguities of status. Aside from Mrs. Fairfax, the three most important of these women are little Adèle Varens, Blanche Ingram, and Grace Poole. All are important negative "role-models" for Jane, and all suggest problems she must overcome before she can reach the independent maturity which is the goal of her pilgrimage.

The first, Adèle, though hardly a woman, is already a "little woman," cunning and doll-like, a sort of sketch for Amy March in Louisa May Alcott's novel. Ostensibly a poor orphan child, like Jane herself, Adèle is evidently the natural daughter of Edward Rochester's dissipated youth. Accordingly, she longs for fashionable gowns rather than for love or freedom, and, the way her mother Céline did, sings and dances for her supper as if she were a clockwork temptress invented by E. T. A. Hoffman. Where Miss Temple's was the way of the lady and Helen's that of the saint, hers and her mother's are the ways of Vanity Fair, ways which have troubled Jane since her days at Gateshead. For how is a poor, plain governess to contend with a society that rewards beauty and style? May not Adèle, the daughter of a "fallen woman," be a model female in a world of prostitutes?

Blanche Ingram, also a denizen of Vanity Fair, presents Jane with a slightly different female image. Tall, handsome, and well-born, she is worldly but, unlike Adèle and Céline, has a respectable place in the world: she is the daughter of "Baroness Ingram of Ingram Park," and—along with Georgiana and Eliza Reed—Jane's classically wicked stepsister. But while Georgiana and Eliza are dismissed to stereotypical fates, Blanche's history teaches Jane ominous lessons. First, the charade of "Bridewell" in which she and Rochester participate relays a secret message: conventional marriage is not only, as the attic implies, a "well" of mystery, it is a Bridewell, a prison, like the Bluebeard's corridor of the third story. Second, the charade of courtship in which Rochester engages her suggests a grim question: is not the game of the marriage "market" a game even scheming women are doomed to lose?

Finally, Grace Poole, the most enigmatic of the women Jane meets at Thornfield—"that mystery of mysteries, as I considered her"—is obviously associated with Bertha, almost as if, with her pint of porter, her "staid and taciturn" demeanor, she were the madwoman's public representative. "Only one hour in the twenty four did she pass with her fellow servants below," Jane notes, attempting to fathom the dark "pool" of the woman's behavior; "all the rest of her time was spent in some low-ceiled, oaken chamber of the third story; there she sat and sewed . . . as companionless as a prisoner in her dungeon" (chap. 17). And that Grace is as companionless as Bertha or Jane herself is undeniably true. Women in Jane's world, acting as agents for men, may be the keepers of other women. But both keepers and prisoners are bound by the same chains. In a sense, then, the mystery of mysteries which Grace Poole suggests to Jane is the mystery of her own life, so that to question Grace's position at Thornfield is to question her own.

Interestingly, in trying to puzzle out the secret of Grace Poole, Jane at one point speculates that Mr. Rochester may once have entertained "tender feelings" for the woman, and when thoughts of Grace's "uncomeliness" seem to refute this possibility, she cements her bond with Bertha's keeper by reminding herself that, after all, "*You* are not beautiful either, and perhaps Mr. Rochester approves you" (chap. 16). Can appearances be trusted? Who is the slave, the master or the servant, the prince or Cinderella? What, in other words, are the real relationships between the master of Thornfield and all these women whose lives revolve around his? None of these questions can, of course, be answered without reference to the central character of the Thornfield episode, Edward Fairfax Rochester.

Jane's first meeting with Rochester is a fairy-tale meeting. Charlotte Brontë deliberately stresses mythic elements: an icy twilight setting out of Coleridge or Fuseli, a rising moon, a great "lion-like" dog gliding through the shadows like "a North-of-England spirit, called a 'Gytrash' which . . . haunted solitary ways, and sometimes came upon belated travellers," followed by "a tall steed, and on its back a rider." Certainly the Romanticized images seem to suggest that universe of male sexuality with which Richard Chase thought the Brontës were obsessed. And Rochester, in a "riding-cloak, fur-collared, and steel-clasped," with "a dark face . . . stern features and a heavy brow" himself appears the very essence of patriarchal energy, Cinderella's prince as a middle-aged warrior (chap. 12). Yet what are we to think of the fact that the prince's first action is to fall on the ice, together with his horse, and exclaim prosaically "What the deuce is to do now?" Clearly the master's mastery is not universal. Jane offers help, and Rochester, leaning on her shoulder, admits that "necessity compels me to make you useful." Later, remembering the scene, he confesses that he too had seen the meeting as a mythic one, though from a perspective entirely other than Jane's. "When you came on me in Hay Lane last night, I . . . had half a mind to demand whether you had bewitched my horse" (chap. 13). Significantly, his playful remark acknowledges *her* powers just as much as (if not more than) her vision of the Gytrash acknowledged *his*. Thus, though in one sense Jane and Rochester begin their relationship as master and servant, prince and Cinderella, Mr. B. and Pamela, in another they begin as spiritual equals.

As the episode unfolds, their equality is emphasized in other scenes as well. For instance, though Rochester imperiously orders Jane to "resume your seat, and answer my questions" while he looks at her drawings, his response to the pictures reveals not only his own Byronic broodings, but his consciousness of hers. "Those eyes in the Evening Star you must have seen in a dream. . . . And who taught you to paint wind? . . . Where did you see Latmos?" (chap. 13). Though such talk would bewilder most of Rochester's other dependents, it is a breath of life to Jane, who begins to fall in love with him not because he is her master but in spite of the fact that he is, not because he is princely in manner, but because, being in some sense her equal, he is the only qualified critic of her art and soul.

Their subsequent encounters develop their equality in even more complex ways. Rudely urged to entertain Rochester, Jane smiles "not a very complacent or submissive smile," obliging her employer to explain that "the fact is, once for all, I don't wish to treat you like an inferior . . . I claim only such superiority as must result from twenty years difference in age and a century's advance in experience" (chap. 14). Moreover, his long account of his adventure with Céline—an account which, incidentally, struck many Victorian readers as totally improper, coming from a dissipated older man to a virginal young governess—emphasizes, at least superficially, not his superiority to Jane but his sense of equality with her. Both Jane and Charlotte Brontë correctly recognize this point, which subverts those Victorian charges: "The ease of his manner," Jane comments, "freed me from painful restraint; the friendly frankness . . . with which he treated me, drew me to him. *I felt at [these] times as if he were my relation rather than my master*" (chap. 15 [ital. ours]). For of course, despite critical suspicions that Rochester is seducing Jane in these scenes, he is, on the contrary, solacing himself with her unseduceable independence in a world of self-marketing Célines and Blanches.

His need for her strength and parity is made clearer soon enough—on, for instance, the occasion when she rescues him from his burning bed (an almost fatally symbolic plight), and later on the occasion when she helps him rescue Richard Mason from the wounds inflicted by "Grace Poole." And that these rescues are facilitated by Jane's and Rochester's mutual sense of equality is made clearest of all in the scene in which only Jane of all the "young ladies" at Thornfield fails to be deceived by Rochester in his gypsy costume:

"With the ladies you must have managed well," she comments, but "You did not act the character of a gypsy with me" (chap. 19). The implication is that he did not—or could not—because he respects "the resolute, wild, free thing looking out of" Jane's eyes as much as she herself does, and understands that just as he can see beyond her everyday disguise as plain Jane the governess, she can see beyond his temporary disguise as a gypsy fortune-teller—or his daily disguise as Rochester the master of Thornfield.

This last point is made again, most explicitly, by the passionate avowals of their first betrothal scene. Beginning with similar attempts at disguise and deception on Rochester's part ("One can't have too much of such a very excellent thing as my beautiful Blanche") that encounter causes Jane in a moment of despair and ire to strip away her own disguises in her most famous assertion of her own integrity:

> "Do you think, because I am poor, obscure, plain, and little, I am soulless and heartless? You think wrong!—I have as much soul as you,—and full as much heart! And if God had gifted me with some beauty, and much wealth, I should have made it as hard for you to leave me, as it is now for me to leave you. I am not talking to you now through the medium of custom, conventionalities, or even of mortal flesh:—it is my spirit that addresses your spirit; just as if both had passed through the grave, and we stood at God's feet equal,—as we are!"
>
> (chap. 23)

Rochester's response is another casting away of disguises, a confession that he has deceived her about Blanche, and an acknowledgment of their parity and similarity: "My bride is here," he admits, "because my *equal* is here, and my *likeness*." The energy informing both speeches is, significantly, not so much sexual as spiritual; the impropriety of its formulation is, as Mrs. Rigby saw, not moral but political, for Charlotte Brontë appears here to have imagined a world in which the prince and Cinderella are democratically equal, Pamela is just as good as Mr. B., master and servant are profoundly alike. And to the marriage of such true minds, it seems, no man or woman can admit impediment.

But of course, as we know, there is an impediment, and that impediment, paradoxically, preexists in both Rochester and Jane, despite their avowals of equality. Though Rochester, for instance, appears in both the gypsy sequence and the betrothal scene to have cast away the disguises that gave him his mastery, it is obviously of some importance that those disguises were necessary in the first place. Why, Jane herself wonders, does Rochester have to trick people, especially women? What secrets are concealed behind the charades he enacts? One answer is surely that he himself senses his trickery is a source of power, and therefore, in Jane's case at least, an evasion of that equality in which he claims to believe. Beyond this, however, it is clear that the secrets Rochester is concealing or disguising throughout much of the book are themselves in Jane's—and Charlotte Brontë's—view secrets of inequality.

The first of these is suggested both by his name, apparently an allusion to the dissolute Earl of Rochester, and by Jane's own reference to the Bluebeard's corridor of the third story: it is the secret of masculine potency, the secret of male sexual guilt. For, like those pre-Byron Byronic heroes the real Restoration Rochester and the mythic Bluebeard (indeed, in relation to Jane, like any experienced adult male), Rochester has specific and "guilty" sexual knowledge which makes him in some sense her "superior." Though this point may seem to contradict the point made earlier about his frankness to Jane, it really should not. Rochester's apparently improper recounting of his sexual adventures *is* a kind of acknowledgment of Jane's equality with him. His possession of the hidden details of sexuality, however—his knowledge, that is, of the *secret* of sex, symbolized both by his doll-like daughter Adèle and by the locked doors of the third story behind which mad Bertha crouches like an animal—qualifies and undermines that equality. And though his puzzling transvestism, his attempt to impersonate a *female* gypsy, may be seen as a semi-conscious effort to reduce this sexual advantage his masculinity gives him (by putting on a woman's clothes he puts on a woman's weakness), both he and Jane obviously recognize the hollowness of such a ruse. The prince is inevitably Cinderella's superior, Charlotte Brontë saw, not because his rank is higher than hers, but because it is *he* who will initiate *her* into the mysteries of the flesh.

That both Jane and Rochester are in some part of themselves conscious of the barrier which Rochester's sexual knowledge poses to their equality is further indicated by the tensions that develop in their relationship after their betrothal. Rochester, having secured Jane's love, almost reflexively begins to treat her as an inferior, a plaything, a virginal possession—for she has now become his initiate, his "mustard-seed," his "little sunny-faced . . . girl-bride." "It is your time now, little tyrant," he declares, "but it will be mine presently: and when once I have fairly seized you, to have and to hold, I'll just—figuratively speaking—attach you to a chain like this" (chap. 24). She, sensing his new sense of power, resolves to keep him "in reasonable check": "I never can bear being dressed like a doll by Mr. Rochester," she remarks, and, more significantly, "I'll not stand you an inch in the stead of a seraglio. . . . I'll [prepare myself] to go out as a missionary to preach liberty to them that are enslaved" (chap. 24). While such assertions have seemed to some critics merely the consequences of Jane's (and Charlotte Brontë's) sexual panic, it should be clear from their context that, as is usual with Jane, they are political rather than sexual statements, attempts at finding emotional strength rather than expressions of weakness.

Finally, Rochester's ultimate secret, the secret that is revealed together with the existence of Bertha, the literal impediment to his marriage with Jane, is another and perhaps most surprising secret of inequality: but this time the hidden facts suggest the master's inferiority rather than his superiority. Rochester, Jane learns, after the aborted wedding ceremony, had married Bertha Mason for status, for sex, for money, for everything but love and equality. "Oh, I have no respect for myself when I think of that act!" he confesses. "An agony of inward contempt masters me. I never loved, I never esteemed, I did not even know her" (chap. 27). And his statement reminds us of Jane's earlier assertion of her own superiority: "I would scorn such a union [as the loveless one he hints he will enter into with Blanche]: therefore I am better than you" (chap. 23). In a sense, then, the most serious crime Rochester has to expiate is not even the crime of exploiting others but the sin of self-exploitation, the sin of Céline and Blanche, to which he, at least, had seemed completely immune.

That Rochester's character and life pose in themselves such substantial impediments to his marriage with Jane does not mean, however, that Jane herself generates none. For one thing, "akin" as she is to Rochester, she suspects him of harboring all the secrets we know he does harbor, and raises defenses against them, manipulating her "master" so as to keep him "in reasonable check." In a larger way, moreover, all the charades and masquerades—the secret messages—of patriarchy have had their effect upon her. Though she loves Rochester the man, Jane has doubts about Rochester the husband even before she learns about Bertha. In her world, she senses, even the equality of love between true minds leads to the inequalities and minor despotisms of marriage. "For a little while," she says cynically to Rochester, "you will perhaps be as you are now, [but] . . . I suppose your love will effervesce in six months, or less. I have observed in books written by men, that period assigned as the farthest to which a husband's ardor extends" (chap. 24). He, of course, vigorously repudiates this prediction, but his argument—"Jane: you please me, and you master me [because] you seem to submit"—implies a kind of Lawrentian sexual tension and only makes things worse. For when he asks "Why do you smile [at this], Jane? What does that inexplicable . . . turn of countenance mean?" her peculiar, ironic smile, reminiscent of Bertha's mirthless laugh, signals an "involuntary" and subtly hostile thought "of Hercules and Samson with their charmers." And that hostility becomes overt at the silk warehouse, where Jane notes that "the more he bought me, the more my cheek burned with a sense of annoyance and degradation. . . . I thought his smile was such as a sultan might, in a blissful and fond moment, bestow on a slave his gold and gems had enriched" (chap. 24).

Jane's whole life-pilgrimage has, of course, prepared her to be angry in this way at Rochester's, and society's, concept of marriage. Rochester's loving tyranny recalls John Reed's unloving despotism, and the erratic nature of Rochester's favors ("in my secret soul I knew that his great kindness to me was balanced by unjust severity to many others" [chap. 15]) recalls Brocklehurst's hypocrisy. But even the dreamlike paintings that Jane produced early in her stay at Thornfield—art works which brought her as close to her "master" as Helen Graham (in *The Tenant of Wildfell Hall*) was to hers—functioned ambiguously, like Helen's, to predict strains in this relationship even while they seemed to be conventional Romantic fantasies. The first represented a drowned female corpse; the second a sort of avenging mother goddess rising (like Bertha Mason Rochester or *Frankenstein*'s monster) in "electric travail" (chap. 13); and the third a terrible paternal specter carefully designed to recall Milton's sinister image of Death. Indeed, this last, says Jane, quoting *Paradise Lost,* delineates "the shape which shape had none," the patriarchal shadow implicit even in the Father-hating gloom of hell.

Given such shadowings and foreshadowings, then, it is no wonder that as Jane's anger and fear about her marriage intensify, she begins to be symbolically drawn back into her own past, and specifically to reexperience the dangerous sense of doubleness that had begun in the red-room. The first sign that this is happening is the powerfully depicted, recurrent dream of a child she begins to have as she drifts into a romance with her master. She tells us that she was awakened "from companionship with this baby-phantom" on the night Bertha attacked Richard Mason, and the next day she is literally called back into the past, back to Gateshead to see the dying Mrs. Reed, who reminds her again of what she once was and potentially still is: "Are you Jane Eyre? . . . I declare she talked to me once like something mad, or like a fiend" (chap. 21). Even more significantly, the phantom-child reappears in two dramatic dreams Jane has on the night before her wedding eve, during which she experiences "a strange regretful consciousness of some barrier dividing" her from Rochester. In the first, "burdened" with the small wailing creature, she is "following the windings of an unknown road" in cold rainy weather, straining to catch up with her future husband but unable to reach him. In the second, she is walking among the ruins of Thornfield, still carrying "the unknown little child" and still following Rochester; as he disappears around "an angle in the road," she tells him, "I bent forward to take a last look; the wall crumbled; I was shaken; the child rolled from my knee, I lost my balance, fell, and woke" (chap. 25).

What are we to make of these strange dreams, or—as Jane would call them—these "presentiments"? To begin with, it seems clear that the wailing child who appears in all of them corresponds to "the poor orphan child" of Bessie's song at Gateshead, and therefore to the child Jane herself, the wailing Cinderella whose pilgrimage began in anger and despair. That child's complaint—"My feet they are sore, and my limbs they are weary; / Long is the way, and the mountains are wild"—is still Jane's, or at least the complaint of that part of her which resists a marriage of inequality. And though consciously Jane wishes to be rid of the heavy problem her orphan self presents, "I might not lay it down anywhere, however tired were my arms, however much its weight impeded my progress." In other words, until she reaches the goal of her pilgrimage—maturity, independence, true equality with Rochester (and therefore in a sense with the rest of the world)—she is doomed to carry her orphaned alter ego everywhere. The burden of the past cannot be sloughed off so easily—not, for instance, by glamorous lovemaking, silk dresses, jewelry, a new name. Jane's "strange regretful consciousness of a barrier" dividing her from Rochester is, thus, a keen though disguised intuition of a problem she herself will pose.

Almost more interesting than the nature of the child image, however, is the *predictive* aspect of the last of the child dreams, the one about the ruin of Thornfield. As Jane correctly foresees, Thornfield *will* within a year become "a dreary ruin, the retreat of bats and owls." Have her own subtle and not-so-subtle hostilities to its master any connection with the catastrophe that is to befall the house? Is her clairvoyant dream in some sense a vision of wish-fulfilment? And why, specifically, is she freed from the burden of the wailing child at the moment *she* falls from Thornfield's ruined wall?

The answer to all these questions is closely related to events which follow upon the child dream. For the apparition of a child in these crucial weeks preceding her marriage is only one symptom of a dissolution of personality Jane seems to be experiencing at this time, a fragmentation of the self comparable to her "syncope" in the red-room. Another symptom appears early in the chapter that begins, anxiously, "there was no putting off the day that advanced— the bridal day" (chap. 25). It is her witty but nervous speculation about the nature of "one Jane Rochester, a person whom as yet I knew not," though "in yonder closet . . . garments *said* to be hers had already displaced [mine]: *for not to me appertained that . . . strange wraith-like apparel*" (chap. 25 [ital. ours]). Again, a third symptom appears on the morning of her wedding: she turns toward the mirror and sees "a robed and veiled figure, so unlike my usual self that it seemed almost the image of a stranger" (chap. 26), reminding us of the moment in the red-room when all had "seemed colder and darker in that visionary hollow" of the looking glass "than in reality." In view of this frightening series of separations within the self— Jane Eyre splitting off from Jane Rochester, the child Jane splitting off from the adult Jane, and the image of Jane weirdly separating from the body of Jane—it is not surprising that another and most mysterious specter, a sort of "vampyre," should appear in the middle of the night to rend and trample the wedding veil of that unknown person, Jane Rochester.

Literally, of course, the nighttime specter is none other than Bertha Mason Rochester. But on a figurative and psychological level it seems suspiciously clear that the specter of Bertha is still another—

indeed the most threatening—avatar of Jane. What Bertha now *does,* for instance, is what Jane wants to do. Disliking the "vapoury veil" of Jane Rochester, Jane Eyre secretly wants to tear the garments up. Bertha does it for her. Fearing the inexorable "bridal day," Jane would like to put it off. Bertha does that for her too. Resenting the new mastery of Rochester, whom she sees as *"dread* but adored," (ital. ours), she wishes to be his equal in size and strength, so that she can battle him in the contest of their marriage. Bertha, "a big woman, in stature almost equalling her husband," has the necessary "virile force" (chap. 26). Bertha, in other words, is Jane's truest and darkest double: she is the angry aspect of the orphan child, the ferocious secret self Jane has been trying to repress ever since her days at Gateshead. For, as Claire Rosenfeld points out, "the novelist who consciously or unconsciously exploits psychological Doubles" frequently juxtaposes "two characters, the one representing the socially acceptable or conventional personality, the other externalizing the free, uninhibited, often criminal self."

It is only fitting, then, that the existence of this criminal self imprisoned in Thornfield's attic is the ultimate legal impediment to Jane's and Rochester's marriage, and that its existence is, paradoxically, an impediment raised by Jane as well as by Rochester. For it now begins to appear, if it did not earlier, that Bertha has functioned as Jane's dark double *throughout* the governess's stay at Thornfield. Specifically, every one of Bertha's appearances—or, more accurately, her manifestations—has been associated with an experience (or repression) of anger on Jane's part. Jane's feelings of "hunger, rebellion, and rage" on the battlements, for instance, were accompanied by Bertha's "low, slow ha! ha!" and "eccentric murmurs." Jane's apparently secure response to Rochester's apparently egalitarian sexual confidences was followed by Bertha's attempt to incinerate the master in his bed. Jane's unexpressed resentment at Rochester's manipulative gypsy-masquerade found expression in Bertha's terrible shriek and her even more terrible attack on Richard Mason. Jane's anxieties about her marriage, and in particular her fears of her own alien "robed and veiled" bridal image, were objectified by the image of Bertha in a "white and straight" dress, "whether gown, sheet, or shroud I cannot tell." Jane's profound desire to destroy Thornfield, the symbol of Rochester's mastery and of her own servitude, will be acted out by Bertha, who burns down the house and destroys *herself* in the process as if she were an agent of Jane's desire as well as her own. And finally, Jane's disguised hostility to Rochester, summarized in her terrifying prediction to herself that "you shall, yourself, pluck out your right eye; yourself cut off your right hand" (chap. 27) comes strangely true through the intervention of Bertha, whose melodramatic death causes Rochester to lose both eye and hand.

These parallels between Jane and Bertha may at first seem somewhat strained. Jane, after all, is poor, plain, little, pale, neat, and quiet, while Bertha is rich, large, florid, sensual, and extravagant; indeed, she was once even beautiful, somewhat, Rochester notes, "in the style of Blanche Ingram." Is she not, then, as many critics have suggested, a monitory image rather than a double for Jane? As Richard Chase puts it, "May not Bertha, Jane seems to ask herself, be a living example of what happens to the woman who [tries] to be the fleshly vessel of the [masculine] *élan?*" "Just as [Jane's] instinct for self-preservation saves her from earlier temptations," Adrienne Rich remarks, "so it must save her from becoming this woman by curbing her imagination at the limits of what is bearable for a powerless woman in the England of the 1840s." Even Rochester himself provides a similar critical appraisal of the relationship between the two. "That is *my wife*," he says, pointing to mad Bertha,

> "And *this* is what I wished to have . . . this young girl who stands so grave and quiet at the mouth of hell, looking collectedly at the gambols of a demon. I wanted her just as a change after that fierce ragout. . . . Compare these clear eyes with the red balls yonder—this face with that mask—this form with that bulk."
>
> (chap. 26)

And of course, in one sense, the relationship between Jane and Bertha is a monitory one: while acting out Jane's secret fantasies, Bertha does (to say the least) provide the governess with an example of how not to act, teaching her a lesson more salutary than any Miss Temple ever taught.

Nevertheless, it is disturbingly clear from recurrent images in the novel that Bertha not only acts *for* Jane, she also acts *like* Jane. The imprisoned Bertha, running "backwards and forwards" on all fours in the attic, for instance, recalls not only Jane the governess, whose only relief from mental pain was to pace "backwards and forwards" in the third story, but also that "bad animal" who was ten-year-old Jane, imprisoned in the red-room, howling and mad. Bertha's "goblin appearance"—"half dream, half reality," says Rochester—recalls the lover's epithets for Jane: "malicious elf," "sprite," "changeling," as well as his playful accusation that she had magically downed his horse at their first meeting. Rochester's description of Bertha as a "monster" ("a fearful voyage I had with such a monster in the vessel" [chap. 27]) ironically echoes Jane's own fear of being a monster ("Am I a monster? . . . is it impossible that Mr. Rochester should have a sincere affection for me?" [chap. 24]). Bertha's fiendish madness recalls Mrs. Reed's remark about Jane ("she talked to me once like something mad or like a fiend") as well as Jane's own estimate of her mental state ("I will hold to the principles received by me when I was sane, and not mad—as I am now" [chap. 27]). And most dramatic of all, Bertha's incendiary tendencies recall Jane's early flaming rages, at Lowood and at Gateshead, as well as that "ridge of lighted heath" which she herself saw as emblematic of her mind in its rebellion against society. It is only fitting, therefore, that, as if to balance the child Jane's terrifying vision of herself as an alien figure in the "visionary hollow" of the red-room looking glass, the adult Jane first clearly perceives her terrible double when Bertha puts on the wedding veil intended for the second Mrs. Rochester, and turns to the mirror. At that moment, Jane sees "the reflection of the visage and features quite distinctly in the dark oblong glass," sees them as if they were her own (chap. 25).

For despite all the habits of harmony she gained in her years at Lowood, we must finally recognize, with Jane herself, that on her arrival at Thornfield she only "*appeared* a disciplined and subdued character*" (ital. ours). Crowned with thorns, finding that she is, in Emily Dickinson's words, "The Wife—without the Sign," she represses her rage behind a subdued facade, but her soul's impulse to dance "like a Bomb, abroad," to quote Dickinson again, has not been exorcised and will not be exorcised until the literal and symbolic death of Bertha frees her from the furies that torment her and makes possible a marriage of equality—makes possible, that is, wholeness within herself. At that point, significantly, when the Bertha in Jane falls from the ruined wall of Thornfield and is destroyed, the orphan child too, as her dream predicts, will roll from her knee—the burden of her past will be lifted—and she will wake. In the meantime, as Rochester says, "never was anything at once so frail and so indomitable . . . consider the resolute wild free thing looking out of [Jane's] eye. . . . Whatever I do with its cage, I cannot get at it—the savage, beautiful creature" (chap. 27).

That the pilgrimage of this "savage, beautiful creature" must now necessarily lead her away from Thornfield is signalled, like many other events in the novel, by the rising of the moon, which accompanies a reminiscent dream of the red-room. Unjustly imprisoned now, as she was then, in one of the traps a patriarchal society provides for outcast Cinderellas, Jane realizes that this time she must escape through deliberation rather than through madness. The maternal moon, admonishing her ("My daughter, flee temptation!") appears to be "a white human form . . . inclining a glorious brow," a strengthening image, as Adrienne Rich suggests, of the Great Mother. Yet—"profoundly, imperiously, archetypal"—this figure has its ambiguities, just as Jane's own personality does, for the last night on which Jane watched such a moon rise was the night Bertha attacked Richard Mason, and the juxtaposition of the two events on that occasion was almost shockingly suggestive:

> [The moon's] glorious gaze roused me. Awaking in the dead of night, I opened my eyes on her disk. . . . It was beautiful, but too solemn: I half rose, and stretched my arm to draw the curtain.
>   Good God! What a cry!
>
> (chap. 20)

Now, as Jane herself recognizes, the moon has elicited from her an act as violent and self-assertive as Bertha's on that night. "What was I?" she thinks, as she steals away from Thornfield. "I had injured—wounded—left my master. I was hateful in my own eyes" (chap. 28). Yet, though her escape may seem as morally ambiguous as the moon's message, it is necessary for her own self-preservation. And soon, like Bertha, she is "crawling forwards on my hands and knees, and then again raised to my feet—as eager and determined as ever to reach the road."

Her wanderings on that road are a symbolic summary of those wanderings of the poor orphan child which constitute her entire life's pilgrimage. For, like Jane's dreams, Bessie's song was an uncannily accurate prediction of things to come. "Why did they send me so far and so lonely, / Up where the moors spread and grey rocks are piled?" Far and lonely indeed Jane wanders, starving, freezing, stumbling, abandoning her few possessions, her name, and even her self-respect in her search for a new home. For "men are hard-hearted, and kind angels only/Watch'd o'er the steps of a poor orphan child." And like the starved wanderings of Hetty Sorel in *Adam Bede,* her terrible journey across the moors suggests the essential homeless-ness—the nameless, placeless, and contingent status—of women in a patriarchal society. Yet because Jane, unlike Hetty, has an inner strength which her pilgrimage seeks to develop, "kind angels" finally do bring her to what is in a sense her true home, the house significantly called *Marsh End* (or Moor House) which is to represent the end of her march toward selfhood. Here she encounters Diana, Mary, and St. John Rivers, the "good" relatives who will help free her from her angry memories of that wicked stepfamily the Reeds. And that the Rivers prove to be literally her relatives is not, in psychological terms, the strained coincidence some readers have suggested. For having left Rochester, having torn off the crown of thorns he offered and repudiated the unequal charade of marriage he proposed, Jane has now gained the strength to begin to discover her real place in the world. St. John helps her find a job in a school, and once again she reviews the choices she has had: "Is it better, I ask, to be a slave in a fool's paradise at Marseilles . . . or to be a village schoolmistress, free and honest, in a breezy mountain nook in the healthy heart of England?" (chap. 31). Her unequivocal conclusion that "I was right when I adhered to principle and law" is one toward which the whole novel seems to have tended.

The qualifying word *seems* is, however, a necessary one. For though in one sense Jane's discovery of her family at Marsh End does represent the end of her pilgrimage, her progress toward selfhood will not be complete until she learns that "principle and law" in the abstract do not always coincide with the deepest principles and laws of her own being. Her early sense that Miss Temple's teachings had merely been superimposed on her native vitality had already begun to suggest this to her. But it is through her encounter with St. John Rivers that she assimilates this lesson most thoroughly. As a number of critics have noticed, all three members of the Rivers family have resonant, almost allegorical names. The names of Jane's true "sisters," Diana and Mary, notes Adrienne Rich, recall the Great Mother in her dual aspects of Diana the huntress and Mary the virgin mother; in this way, as well as through their independent, learned, benevolent personalities, they suggest the ideal of female strength for which Jane has been searching. St. John, on the other hand, has an almost blatantly patriarchal name, one which recalls both the masculine abstraction of the gospel according to St. John ("in the beginning was the *Word*") and the disguised misogyny of St. John the Baptist, whose patristic and evangelical contempt for the flesh manifested itself most powerfully in a profound contempt for the *female*. Like Salome, whose rebellion against such misogyny Oscar Wilde was later also to associate with the rising moon of female power, Jane must symbolically, if not literally, behead the abstract principles of this man before she can finally achieve her true independence.

At first, however, it seems that St. John is offering Jane a viable alternative to the way of life proposed by Rochester. For where Rochester, like his dissolute namesake, ended up appearing to offer a life of pleasure, a path of roses (albeit with concealed thorns), and a marriage of passion, St. John seems to propose a life of principle, a path of thorns (with no concealed roses), and a marriage of spirituality. His self-abnegating rejection of the worldly beauty Rosamund Oliver—another character with a strikingly resonant name—is disconcerting to the passionate and Byronic part of Jane, but at least it shows that, unlike hypocritical Brocklehurst, he practices what he preaches. And what he preaches is the Carlylean sermon of self-actualization through work: "Work while it is called today, for the night cometh wherein no man can work." If she follows him, Jane realizes, she will substitute a divine Master for the master she served at Thornfield, and replace love with labor—for "you are formed for labour, not for love," St. John tells her. Yet when, long ago at Lowood, she asked for "a new servitude" was not some such solution half in her mind? When, pacing the battlements at Thornfield she insisted that "women [need] a field for their efforts as much as their brothers do" (chap. 12), did she not long for some such practical "exercise"? "Still will my Father with promise and blessing,/Take to his bosom the poor orphaned child," Bessie's song had predicted. Is not Marsh End, then, the promised end, and St. John's way the way to His bosom?

Jane's early repudiation of the spiritual harmonies offered by Helen Burns and Miss Temple is the first hint that, while St. John's way will tempt her, she must resist it. That, like Rochester, he is "akin" to her is clear. But where Rochester represents the fire of her nature, her cousin represents the ice. And while for some women ice may "suffice," for Jane, who has struggled all her life, like a sane version of Bertha, against the polar cold of a loveless world, it clearly will not. As she falls more deeply under St. John's "freezing spell," she realizes increasingly that to please him "I must disown half my

nature." And "as his wife," she reflects, she would be "always restrained . . . forced to keep the fire of my nature continually low,
. . . though the imprisoned flame consumed vital after vital" (chap.
34). In fact, as St. John's wife and "the sole helpmate [he] can influence efficiently in life, and retain absolutely till death" (chap. 34), she
will be entering into a union even more unequal than that proposed
by Rochester, a marriage reflecting, once again, her absolute exclusion from the life of wholeness toward which her pilgrimage has
been directed. For despite the integrity of principle that distinguishes
him from Brocklehurst, despite his likeness to "the warrior Greatheart, who guards his pilgrim convoy from the onslaught of Apol-
lyon" (chap. 38), St. John is finally, as Brocklehurst was, a pillar of
patriarchy, "a cold cumbrous column" (chap. 34). But where Brocklehurst had removed Jane from the imprisonment of Gateshead only
to immure her in a dank valley of starvation, and even Rochester had
tried to make her the "slave of passion," St. John wants to imprison
the "resolute wild free thing" that is her soul in the ultimate cell, the
"iron shroud" of principle (chap. 34).

Though in many ways St. John's attempt to "imprison" Jane
may seem the most irresistible of all, coming as it does at a time
when she is congratulating herself on just that adherence to "principle and law" which he recommends, she escapes from his fetters
more easily than she had escaped from either Brocklehurst or Rochester. Figuratively speaking, this is a measure of how far she has
traveled in her pilgrimage toward maturity. Literally, however, her
escape is facilitated by two events. First, having found what is, despite all its ambiguities, her true family, Jane has at last come into her
inheritance. Jane Eyre is now the heir of that uncle in Madeira whose
first intervention in her life had been, appropriately, to define the
legal impediment to her marriage with Rochester, now literally as
well as figuratively an independent woman, free to go her own way
and follow her own will. But her freedom is also signaled by a second event: the death of Bertha.

Her first "presentiment" of that event comes, dramatically, as
an answer to a prayer for guidance. St. John is pressing her to reach
a decision about his proposal of marriage. Believing that "I had now
put love out of the question, and thought only of duty," she "entreats
Heaven" to "Show me, show me the path." As always at major moments in Jane's life, the room is filled with moonlight, as if to remind
her that powerful forces are still at work both without and within

her. And now, because such forces are operating, she at last hears—
she is receptive to—the bodiless cry of Rochester: "Jane! Jane! Jane!"
Her response is an immediate act of self-assertion. "I broke from St.
John. . . . It was *my* time to assume ascendancy. *My* powers were in
play and in force" (chap. 35). But her sudden forcefulness, like her
"presentiment" itself, is the climax of all that has gone before. Her
new and apparently telepathic communion with Rochester, which
many critics have seen as needlessly melodramatic, has been made
possible by her new independence and Rochester's new humility.
The plot device of the cry is merely a sign that the relationship for
which both lovers had always longed is now possible, a sign that
Jane's metaphoric speech of the first betrothal scene has been trans-
lated into reality: "my spirit . . . addresses your spirit, just as if both
had passed through the grave, and we stood at God's feet, equal—as
we are!" (chap. 23). For to the marriage of Jane's and Rochester's true
minds there is now, as Jane unconsciously guesses, no impediment.

Jane's return to Thornfield, her discovery of Bertha's death and
of the ruin her dream had predicted, her reunion at Ferndean with
the maimed and blinded Rochester, and their subsequent marriage
form an essential epilogue to that pilgrimage toward selfhood which
had in other ways concluded at Marsh End, with Jane's realization
that she could not marry St. John. At that moment, "the wondrous
shock of feeling had come like the earthquake which shook the foun-
dations of Paul and Silas' prison; it had opened the doors of the soul's
cell, and loosed its bands—it had wakened it out of its sleep" (chap.
36). For at that moment she had been irrevocably freed from the
burden of her past, freed both from the raging specter of Bertha
(which had already fallen in fact from the ruined wall of Thornfield)
and from the self-pitying specter of the orphan child (which had
symbolically, as in her dream, rolled from her knee). And at that
moment, again as in her dream, she had *wakened* to her own self, her
own needs. Similarly, Rochester, "caged eagle" that he seems (chap.
37), has been freed from what was for him the burden of Thornfield,
though at the same time he appears to have been fettered by the
injuries he received in attempting to rescue Jane's mad double from
the flames devouring his house. That his "fetters" pose no impediment to a new marriage, that he and Jane are now, in reality, equals,
is the thesis of the Ferndean section.

Many critics, starting with Richard Chase, have seen Rochester's injuries as "a symbolic castration," a punishment for his early

profligacy and a sign that Charlotte Brontë (as well as Jane herself), fearing male sexual power, can only imagine marriage as a union with a diminished Samson. "The tempo and energy of the universe can be quelled, we see, by a patient, practical woman," notes Chase ironically. And there is an element of truth in this idea. The angry Bertha in Jane *had* wanted to punish Rochester, to burn him in his bed, destroy his house, cut off his hand and pluck out his overmastering "full falcon eye." Smiling enigmatically, she had thought of "Hercules and Samson, with their charmers."

It had not been her goal, however, to quell "the tempo and energy of the universe," but simply to strengthen herself, to make herself an equal of the world Rochester represents. And surely another important symbolic point is implied by the lovers' reunion at Ferndean: when both were physically whole they could not, in a sense, *see* each other because of the social disguises—master/servant, prince/Cinderella—blinding them, but now that those disguises have been shed, now that they are equals, they can (though one is blind) see and speak even beyond the medium of the flesh. Apparently sightless, Rochester—in the tradition of blinded Gloucester—now sees more clearly than he did when as a "mole-eyed blockhead" he married Bertha Mason (chap. 27). Apparently mutilated, he is paradoxically stronger than he was when he ruled Thornfield, for now, like Jane, he draws his powers from within himself, rather than from inequity, disguise, deception. Then, at Thornfield, he was "no better than the old lightning-struck chestnut tree in the orchard," whose ruin foreshadowed the catastrophe of his relationship with Jane. Now, as Jane tells him, he is "green and vigorous. Plants will grow about your roots whether you ask them or not" (chap. 37). And now, being equals, he and Jane can afford to depend upon each other with no fear of one exploiting the other.

Nevertheless, despite the optimistic portrait of an egalitarian relationship that Brontë seems to be drawing here, there is "a quiet autumnal quality" about the scenes at Ferndean, as Robert Bernard Martin points out. The house itself, set deep in a dark forest, is old and decaying: Rochester had not even thought it suitable for the loathsome Bertha, and its valley-of-the-shadow quality makes it seem rather like a Lowood, a school of life where Rochester must learn those lessons Jane herself absorbed so early. As a dramatic setting, moreover, Ferndean is notably stripped and asocial, so that the physical isolation of the lovers suggests their spiritual isolation in a world where such egalitarian marriages as theirs are rare, if not impossible. True minds, Charlotte Brontë seems to be saying, must withdraw into a remote forest, a wilderness even, in order to circumvent the strictures of a hierarchal society.

Does Brontë's rebellious feminism—that "irreligious" dissatisfaction with the social order noted by Miss Rigby and *Jane Eyre*'s other Victorian critics—compromise itself in this withdrawal? Has Jane exorcised the rage of orphanhood only to retreat from the responsibilities her own principles implied? Tentative answers to these questions can be derived more easily from *The Professor, Shirley,* and *Villette* than from *Jane Eyre,* for the qualified and even (as in *Villette*) indecisive endings of Brontë's other novels suggest that she herself was unable clearly to envision viable solutions to the problem of patriarchal oppression. In all her books, writing . . . in a sort of trance, she was able to act out that passionate drive toward freedom which offended agents of the status quo, but in none was she able consciously to define the full meaning of achieved freedom—perhaps because no one of her contemporaries, not even a Wollstonecraft or a Mill, could adequately describe a society so drastically altered that the matured Jane and Rochester could really live in it.

What Brontë could not logically define, however, she could embody in tenuous but suggestive imagery and in her last, perhaps most significant redefinitions of Bunyan. Nature in the largest sense seems now to be on the side of Jane and Rochester. *Ferndean,* as its name implies, is without artifice—"no flowers, no garden-beds"— but it is green as Jane tells Rochester he will be, green and ferny and fertilized by soft rains. Here, isolated from society but flourishing in a natural order of their own making, Jane and Rochester will become physically "bone of [each other's] bone, flesh of [each other's] flesh" (chap. 38), and here the healing powers of nature will eventually restore the sight of one of Rochester's eyes. Here, in other words, nature, unleashed from social restrictions, will do "no miracle—but her best" (chap. 35). For not the Celestial City but a natural paradise, the country of Beulah "upon the borders of heaven," where "the contract between bride and bridegroom [is] renewed," has all along been, we now realize, the goal of Jane's pilgrimage.

As for the Celestial City itself, Charlotte Brontë implies here (though she will later have second thoughts) that such a goal is the dream of those who accept inequities on earth, one of the many tools used by patriarchal society to keep, say, governesses in their "place."

Because she believes this so deeply, she quite consciously concludes *Jane Eyre* with an allusion to *Pilgrim's Progress* and with a half-ironic apostrophe to that apostle of celestial transcendence, that shadow of "the warrior Greatheart," St. John Rivers. "His," she tells us, "is the exaction of the apostle, who speaks but for Christ when he says— 'Whosoever will come after me, let him deny himself and take up his cross and follow me'" (chap. 38). For it was, finally, to repudiate such a crucifying denial of the self that Brontë's "hunger, rebellion, and rage" led her to write *Jane Eyre* in the first place and to make it an "irreligious" redefinition, almost a parody, of John Bunyan's vision. And the astounding progress toward equality of plain Jane Eyre, whom Miss Rigby correctly saw as "the personification of an unregenerate and undisciplined spirit," answers by its outcome the bitter question Emily Dickinson was to ask fifteen years later: "'My husband'—women say—/Stroking the Melody—/Is *this*—the way?" No, Jane declares in her flight from Thornfield, *that* is not the way. *This,* she says—this marriage of true minds at Ferndean—this is the way. Qualified and isolated as her way may be, it is at least an emblem of hope. Certainly Charlotte Brontë was never again to indulge in quite such an optimistic imagining.

Jane Eyre in Search of Her Story

Rosemarie Bodenheimer

On the first page of *Jane Eyre,* Jane is ordered to keep silent; at the end of the novel her voice becomes the central source of perception for her blind and captive audience, Mr. Rochester, "impressing by sound on his ear what light could no longer stamp on his eye." How Jane acquires and uses the power of speech, and with whom, are subjects that bear both upon the story of her development as a character and upon the first-person narrative stance that Charlotte Brontë invented for her first successful novel. At many points in the telling, Jane's story calls attention to the questions, "How shall I learn to tell the story of my life?" and "What kind of a story is it?" And her narrative is persistently set in relation to other, more conventional kinds of stories—not only the fairy tales, Gothics, and "governess tales" which have received critical attention, but also the internal, interpolated narratives like Rochester's story about his affair with Céline Varens, St. John Rivers's version of Jane's inheritance story, or the innkeeper's tale about the burning of Thornfield. Jane's insistence on the originality of her character and voice must therefore be seen as taking shape in a world full of fictions, which often prove to be in curiously unstable relations with her own.

"Until you can speak pleasantly, remain silent," Mrs. Reed says to Jane in the opening scene; the words quite precisely reverse Brontë's private formulation of the heroics of narration:

From *Papers on Language and Literature* 16, no. 4 (Fall 1980). © 1980 by the Board of Trustees, Southern Illinois University.

> The standard heroes and heroines of novels are personages
> in whom I could never from childhood upwards take an
> interest, believe to be natural, or wish to imitate. Were I
> obliged to copy these characters I would simply not write
> at all. . . . Unless I have the courage to use the language
> of Truth in preference to the jargon of Conventionality, I
> ought to be silent.

And, in fact, Jane Eyre's history may be read as the story of an em-
powered narrator, which describes her gradual, though partial release from conventional bondages, both social and fictional. Such a
reading, emphasizing the literary self-consciousness of *Jane Eyre,*
shows that the "problem" of speaking out in a single and singular
voice is not only Brontë's narrative voice, but an explicit and com-
plexly argued theme in the substance of the fiction.

In one of the moments so frequent in self-conscious narratives,
Brontë gives us an embedded image of the fiction-maker herself.
Restless at Thornfield, believing in "the existence of other and more
vivid kinds of goodness," Jane stands on the roof of Rochester's
house and indulges the "bright visions" of her imagination,

> to let my heart be heaved by the exultant movement,
> which, while it swelled it in trouble, expanded it with life;
> and, best of all, to open my inward ear to a tale that was
> never ended—a tale my imagination created, and narrated
> continuously; quickened with all of incident, life, fire,
> feeling, that I desired and had not in my actual existence.

The temptation to read this as an uncritical image of Jane's all-
devouring fantasy has been well argued away by critics who show
how little we can identify Jane's romantic daydreams with the vision
of the novel. But the passage raises a number of points which have,
finally, to be understood in the entire context of Jane's role as the
teller of her life. First, the creations of Jane's imagination have already been made suspect during the childhood scene in the red-
room, where her fantasies overwhelm and overpower her. The scene
of Jane's Thornfield fantasy life—pacing the third story, within ear-
shot of the mysterious laughter—links it, as well, with the inarticu-
late sounds that signify Bertha Mason's imprisonment in her own
passions. The inward tale is clearly presented as a substitute for the
life of social observation and action that Jane wants; and as soon as a

real relation presents itself—as Rochester conveniently does two pages on—Jane stops needing the relief, though she does not stop the habit of transforming actual experience into narrative.

But it is exactly the curious conflation of heroine, teller, and audience that is crucial to the state Jane describes, and that makes it an image of imprisonment rather than one of romantic escape. This tale, a transaction between Jane's "imagination" and her "inward ear," is inaudible, untestable; it seems to have no beginning or end because of its function as daydream, and because there is no audience. Jane's progress in the novel is in opposition to this state, and has to do with finding a fit audience for whom she can give a proper shape to her own story.

Much of the drama in the Gateshead section of the novel is created through the tension between Jane's—and our—listening in outraged silence to the versions of her offered by members of the Reed household, and Jane's explosive outbreaks into speech. The novel begins where it does to emphasize exactly this: "that day" so casually introduced in the first sentence is the day on which Jane first talks back to John Reed, her accustomed and quite involuntary words articulating "parallels" drawn "in silence, which I never thought thus to have declared aloud." Jane's frantic comparison of John Reed with the Roman emperors of her reading is comic, and lightly suggests the imbalance between her interior life and social reality that results from her long-withheld resentment. The immediate effect of the outbreak is the famous red-room scene, which teaches Jane that passion vented leads to imprisonment—a major theme of the novel. Yet the real climax of the Gateshead section is the scene in which Jane lashes out at Mrs. Reed, achieving a taste of the power of speech and a brief sensation of victory. That scene gathers up many of the implications of "tale-telling" as it is treated in the first section.

Jane's pain and confusion is established from the beginning as a response to the disjunction between the descriptions she must listen to and the truth of her character. Her first spoken words are, "What does Bessie say I have done?" Requiring evidence for crime, and getting none, she has already a touch of skepticism about the accuracy even of the relation between Bessie's saying and her own doing. Mrs. Reed's culminating blow is to publicize Jane to Brocklehurst as a liar. The accusation could not be more wrong; it attacks Jane at her tenderest spot, on the matter of false and true speaking. Her subsequent outburst at Mrs. Reed is finally effective at quenching her antagonist

because Jane asserts for the first time a reciprocal power of tale-
telling, and an equivalent power to defame Mrs. Reed's character: "I
will tell anybody who asks me questions this exact tale. . . . I'll let
everybody at Lowood know what you are, and what you have
done." The triumph in a victory won with weapons of the oppressor
is soon corroded, and the narrator makes a statement that sets up for
the next stage of Jane's learning: "I would fain exercise some better
faculty than that of fierce speaking." It has become necessary that
Jane find a life, and a way of telling it, that does not equate truth-
telling with revenge.

Though less dramatic than the "fierce speaking" sequence, Jane's
relationships with Mr. Lloyd and Bessie are also full of attention to
how she talks. The doctor is Jane's first sympathetic audience, but
the narrative emphasis during his dialogue with her is on her inepti-
tude at putting her woes into words. During the first half of the
scene Bessie answers for Jane most of the time, frustrating our desire
for Jane to take charge of her own story; when the doctor maneuvers
Bessie's departure, the narrative pauses to announce the importance
of the theme: "Children can feel, but they cannot analyze their feelings; and if the analysis is partially effected in thought, they know
not how to express the result of the process in words." Jane's "bun-
gling" pauses and "meagre" truths are meant to show again the imbalance between Jane's words and her thoughts and so to establish
the terms for her future growth. A similar focus on Jane's way of
talking informs her dialogue with Bessie after the outburst at Mrs.
Reed; here Jane dares more gentle frankness, with more reward, than
ever before, and Bessie exclaims, "You little sharp thing! you've got
quite a new way of talking."

Once at Lowood, Jane has a "story," and how she tells it becomes an explicit issue. Helen Burns is Jane's first literary critic. To
her, Jane pours out "the tale of my sufferings and resentments. Bitter
and truculent when excited, I spoke as I felt, without reserve or soft-
ening." She then expects Helen to agree to her tale's moral: " 'Well,'
I asked impatiently, 'is not Mrs. Reed a hard-hearted, bad woman?' "
Helen chastises Jane for wasting her energy "registering wrongs";
she makes it clear that the tale-teller chooses her story. Though Hel-
en's own focus on heaven is never Jane's own, Helen's admonitions
modify Jane's tale when she comes to tell it to Miss Temple. The
description of that process is fascinating for its emphasis on art and
credibility:

I resolved in the depth of my heart that I would be most moderate: most correct; and, having reflected a few minutes in order to arrange coherently what I had to say, I told her all the story of my sad childhood. Exhausted by emotion, my language was more subdued than it generally was when it developed that sad theme; and mindful of Helen's warnings against the indulgence of resentment, I infused into the narrative far less of gall and wormwood than ordinary. Thus restrained and simplified, it sounded more credible: I felt as I went on that Miss Temple fully believed me.

The episode marks the socialization of Jane's narrative style; the moment when she realizes the power of conscious control over sequence, diction, and tone. Unlike the warlike power to threaten that she uses with Mrs. Reed, this deliberate restraint gets her what she has always wanted: the power to make others believe her. It is especially important here that at the moment when Jane's internal life finally finds a fair hearing, Brontë should stress the complicated artfulness required by Jane's double awareness of story and listener, the interdependence of art and audience. At the same moment, however, Brontë offers to us—her audience—a similarly double position, for we have experienced the rage as well as the restraint; and are allowed to feel the difference between the "credible story" Miss Temple hears and the personal sources or original truths of the experiences themselves. In this way a crucial tension is established between Jane's moral progress in designing her story and the novel's implicit assertion that "truth" is not credibility, that it is made of different, less coherent stuff. My point here is less to emphasize Brontë's own ambivalence about "Truth versus Art" than to point out her artfulness in setting up the dialectic between Jane's "internal" progress as a narrator and the "external" narrative, which creates in the reader a dramatic sense of the tension. As audience to Jane's audiences, we are required to maintain a strenuous consciousness of the pressures in the process of turning experience into story.

Jane's primary audience is Rochester; in that relationship the dynamic of "fierce speaking and credible narrative" is revived and expanded. The "rightness" of Rochester as Jane's lover is initially dramatized through Jane's freedom to speak frankly with him and their shared distrust of conventional social languages. This is made

plain in the opening of one of their important early dialogues when
Rochester asks Jane if she thinks him handsome. Her response sets
up both the beauty of the relationship and its danger: "I should, if I
had deliberated, have replied to this question by something conventionally vague and polite; but the answer somehow slipped from my
tongue before I was aware:—'No sir.'" The dialogue (which is,
again, about the subject of how Jane and Rochester are to speak)
becomes the brusque flirtation which is to characterize and validate
the love affair; but the involuntary aspect of Jane's answer is a two-
sided token, recalling her helpless, uncontrolled early outbursts as
well as offering a new freedom. The manipulative character of Rochester's power to move Jane to involuntary speech is underlined in his
attempt to trick her into self-revelation by disguising himself as a
gypsy fortune-teller; and it comes to a head in the garden proposal
scene when he successfully precipitates Jane into speech by threatening her with jealousy and loss. The moment echoes Jane's scene
with Mrs. Reed ("*Speak* I must: I had been trodden on severely, and
must turn: but how?"; Jane is again mastered by repressed feelings:
"In listening, I sobbed convulsively; for I could repress what I endured no longer: I was obliged to yield; and I was shaken from head
to foot with acute distress. . . . The vehemence of emotion, stirred
by grief and love within me, was claiming mastery, and struggling
for full sway; and asserting a right to predominate: to overcome, to
live, rise, and reign at last; yes,—and to speak."

"Raised to something like passion," Jane asserts her equality
with Rochester in a new kind of "fierce speaking." Interestingly, the
idea of freedom arises, again, from that stance: "I have spoken my
mind, and go anywhere now. . . . I am a free human being with an
independent will; which I now exert to leave you." It is a rehearsal in
miniature for her later actual leaving, after another fervent moment
of speaking her mind releases her to do what she knows to be necessary for the preservation of her integrity. The recurrent conjunction of impassioned speech and liberation from a social tie is an important one. "Speaking the mind" is not storytelling; it lacks the
artistic control and the awareness of audience that precede social in-
tegration. The opposition between these two kinds of speech is crucial to an understanding of Jane's final return to Rochester.

At the end of the novel, Rochester's blindness leaves Jane in sole
command of the narrative field; she becomes the single source of
evidence, the voice which tells what her audience cannot see, and the

arbiter of what is and is not to be told. This rather absolute overturning of the power situation at the end of the novel has generated a good deal of critical eyebrow-raising. Of course it is true that Brontë defines relationships as power struggles, that her imagination tends to work between extreme poles. But it is hardly an imagination that knows not what it does. The narrative here is completely forthright about Jane's new position: "His countenance reminded one of a lamp quenched, waiting to be relit—and alas! it was not himself that could now kindle the lustre of animated expression: he was dependent on another for that office! I had meant to be gay and careless, but the powerlessness of that strong man touched me to the quick." What Brontë is interested in dramatizing in the last scenes is not that Jane has the power, but how she is to use it. And the power she takes to "rehumanize" and "rekindle" is defined precisely as the power of storytelling.

When Jane first sees Rochester at Ferndean, she immediately describes her reactions in terms of the restraint associated with "credible narrative": "I had no difficulty in restraining my voice from exclamation, my step from hasty advance." She arranges, of course, that Rochester recognize her by her voice. Most importantly, she manipulates the telling of her adventures in ways which are carefully designed to "cure" Rochester's despair; she becomes "the instrument for his cure," not in the way he had earlier intended, but through the powers of the storyteller to move her audience. On the first night, she gives "very partial replies" to his questions because she wishes "to open no fresh well of emotion in his heart: my sole present aim was to cheer him." She banks on the suspense of a half-told tale to keep his hopes going overnight, and so realizes the power at her command: "'I see I have the means of fretting him out of his melancholy for some time to come.'" Her presentation of her relationship with St. John draws out the suspense to exactly that end; while Jane plays on Rochester's jealousy as he had earlier played on hers, she does so with a full moral control of its effect. "The narrative of my experience" is "softened considerably" to avoid inflicting "unnecessary pain"; and in that description we hear the final stage of the mediation between "truth" and "audience" that Jane began to learn in telling her story to Miss Temple. Having then discovered art as a means to credibility, she now uses it for the moral and emotional amusement, relief, and animation of her audience.

Brontë's interest in stressing Jane's responsibility to her audience is particularly clear when she makes a special point of telling us that Jane withholds the "supernatural" experience of hearing Rochester's voice calling her. Even though she has earlier proclaimed the belief that the event was nature doing "her best," Jane feels that Rochester's tendency to "gloom, needed not the deeper shade of the supernatural." The passage seals Jane's commitment to "credible narrative," and to the shaping and pruning of experience that it demands. The implication for her development is clear: Jane has grown up into a purveyor of tales realistic and moral, suspenseful and heartwarming. Since the time of her lonely pacing in Thornfield's third story, her tale has acquired form and social content, while she has acquired an endless supply of audience and the concomitant power and responsibility to shape a vision of the world for him.

A private and dependent audience of one in a secluded manor may not seem so triumphant a development from that internal continuous narrative—though it is not a bad image for the single and private relationship of novelist and reader. But in Jane's career the search for audience is essentially a search for love and human connection. And maintaining the connection means withholding some truths. Thus, the act of withholding so curiously stressed at the end of the novel is a guarantee of the social connection of Jane and Rochester, even as it suppresses the mystic connection implied by the supernatural calls through the night. It is Jane's assertion of control, both over Rochester and over forces in the universe, and in the psyche, that belie the desire to shape and control experience.

While the "internal" plot presents Jane's repression as a moral choice, the larger narrative remains in command of both the shapely story and what it leaves out. Jane is represented as having been moved to find Rochester by that "supernatural" event for which she claims full reality; the fact that she rejects it as material to be told to Rochester shows again the tension between Brontë's character and her narrative, which retrieves and includes the irrational sources that Jane learns to repress in order to achieve her social, loving, and controlling ends. If Jane grows up to be a successful narrator, she is not—at least not yet—the narrator of *Jane Eyre,* whose vision depends on the tense truth of the discontinuity between fierce feeling and credible story.

Brontë's linkage of controlled, artful narrative with loving sociality also takes the more negative form of a linkage between stereotypical social behavior and recognizably conventional narrative modes. Conventional characters think of their lives as conventional stories; in this way they are effectively deprived of inner reality. Against that world of social and narrative convention, Jane devotes herself to the notion of originality, which becomes, in her hands, a moral attribute.

Brontë continually asks us to think about typical plots in order to disengage them from her own. Georgiana and Eliza Reed function, for example, as parody heroines of other and lesser stories. After relating the history of Jane's parents (in a paragraph that is a masterpiece of conventional plot summary, complete with wife "cut off without a shilling") Bessie and Abbot decide that "a beauty like Miss Georgiana" would be a more "moving" heroine of that tale than Jane could be. And Georgiana herself tries to see her life in novelistic conventions; when Jane revisits Gateshead at the time of Mrs. Reed's death, Georgiana confides in her: "in short, a volume of a novel of fashionable life was that day improvised by her for my benefit." Eliza parodies, in a different way, the choice of religious sacrifice more seriously depicted in the careers of Helen Burns and St. John Rivers. But those stories too—and it is notable that the novel ends with St. John's—function as roads not taken, choices against which the originality of Jane's history is to take form.

The moral status of originality is also apparent in Jane's judgments. Her indictment of Blanche Ingram takes this form: "She was not good; she was not original: she used to repeat sounding phrases from books; she never offered, nor had, an opinion of her own." The sentimental phrases with which the other ladies of the Thornfield party respond to the stranger Mason are also used as evidence against their powers of accurate moral judgment. Even the banality of charming Rosamond Oliver is most effectively set in the observation that she imagines that Jane's "previous history, if known, would make a delightful romance."

Jane's own story is forever veering into one or another recognizable literary mode, only to be brought up short in a comic deflation. A few examples must stand in for the rest: when Jane is nervously waiting in the Millcote Inn for a carriage to take her to Thornfield for the first time, the moment of uncertainty brings on the rather grandiose diction of adventure: "It is a very strange sensation to inexperienced youth to feel itself quite alone in the world: cut adrift from every connection; uncertain whether the port to which it is bound can be reached, and prevented by many impediments from returning to that which it has quitted." After waiting an unheroic half-hour, Jane ventures to ring the bell, only to find that the carriage is already there, responsibly waiting. In a similar and more central moment, Rochester's entrance is elaborately, romantically set in a description of the landscape—and the hero's first act is to fall down in the middle of it. Later, after the first major burst of "Gothic," the fire set to Rochester's bed, Jane's practical efforts wake him, "fulminating strange anathemas at finding himself lying in a pool of water. 'Is there a flood?' he cried." The language is a literal douse of comedy, acting like the others to jolt characters and reader out of that other sort of story into which we have, momentarily, been lulled.

In its most direct form, the standard of originality is used to deny a full life to the minor characters by having them think of themselves as "characters" in bad fictions. Yet this quiet but constant undertow of concern to claim originality for Jane's character and narrative actually takes the form of using, then apparently disengaging from, literary models, as though the only possibility of originality in a world full of other stories were the ability to draw back and recognize them as conventions. The stance is really a dependent position of independence; but it is certainly a self-conscious one, containing and making a subject of the stresses Brontë must have felt as she worked out the narrative of *Jane Eyre* in full awareness of the conventional fictions she scorned.

The sorts of stories that Jane does not tell herself are put into the mouths of other characters. These narratives within the narrative work as measures for Jane's art, and also raise questions about exactly what kind of a story Jane's life might be. Rochester is, of course, the most important secondary narrator. At first he is represented as a deserving lover because of his own unconventionality and because his interest in Jane is sparked by his sense that she is "singular." In the central portion of the novel, however, his ways of describing his life, and Jane's role in it, show a desperate reliance on conventional stories which are used to mask the "true story" of his marriage.

When Rochester appears at Thornfield, he conceals a history which makes him "interesting"—a word which shares honors with "original" throughout the novel. The narrative in the Thornfield section is set up to engage both Jane and the reader in working out the solution to Rochester's mystery; at this point Jane herself has no comparable "interesting story" to speak of. Jane is offered a series of evasive accounts before she finally hears Rochester's own truthful narrative on the night of the intended wedding day. The first narrative, Mrs. Fairfax's, suggests that Rochester's story is one about the trials of a second son in a proud, wealthy family. The second, Rochester's story of his affair with Céline Varens, begins with a piece of ironic apology for having been so conventional: "In short, I began the process of ruining myself in the received style; like any other spoonie. I had not, it seems, the originality to chalk out a new road to shame and destruction, but trode the old track with stupid exactness not to deviate an inch from the beaten centre." Rochester is capable of as much literary self-consciousness about the telling of his life as Jane is herself. Yet the tale of Céline is in fact full of conventional language, and is organized to show that Rochester's cynical rendition of that cheap melodrama is actually a digressive maneuver. The expostulations to Thornfield which burst out in his dramatic interruption reveal that he is inwardly writing quite another tale—"arranging a point with my destiny"—that concerns him far more deeply: the story of a bigamous marriage.

The sense that Jane is living amidst a set of manufactured tales becomes explicit in her dialogue with Grace Poole after the fire in Rochester's bed; Grace's version of what has happened is designed to make Jane doubt the evidence of her senses and to write her out of the story. Rochester's house party stages a novel of fashionable life in an episode which is saturated on every level of narrative with theatrical metaphor. It is the final, major production in the series of cover stories—except, of course, for the proposed wedding to Jane. All of these incidents demonstrate Rochester's belief that he can arrange his destiny, act simultaneously as production manager and fortune-teller, and write both the beginnings and the ends of his life plans as though they were stories. In every case, his scenes are interrupted by extrusions of his real "story," the marriage with Bertha. In this carefully orchestrated presentation of Rochester as narrator, or playwright, the linkage between conventional plots and untruthfulness is firmly forged.

Rochester's ways of imagining Jane in his projected romance also show how he betrays his own recognition of Jane's originality; in attempting to describe his feeling about Jane's place in his life, he falls into traditional or fashionable modes of fantasy. When he tries to load Jane with clothes and jewels, his words debase even the notion of originality itself. In an exchange remarkable for its explicit "story" metaphors, Jane protests Rochester's possessive looks: " 'You need not look in that way;' I said: 'if you do, I'll wear nothing but my old Lowood frocks to the end of the chapter.' " Rochester answers as though Jane were the latest fashionable delight of the social stage: " 'Oh, it is rich to see and hear her! . . . Is she original? Is she piquant? I would not exchange this one little English girl for the grand Turk's whole seraglio; gazelle-eyes, houri-forms and all!' " In the context established, he could hardly commit a more devastating lapse of imagination as to the kind of story he might compare Jane's to. At other moments, Jane is a combination of fairy-elf and heavenly messenger ("the instrument for my cure,"), presumably in a spiritualized version of the reformed rake's tale.

Brontë underlines the irresponsibility of this state of mind in the fairy tale Rochester tells Adèle about "taking mademoiselle to the moon." Adèle will have none of it; she points out that Rochester will be depriving Jane of food, clothing, and shelter. It is a lovely narrative move, suggesting the sinister undercurrents of fantasy-play that even a child can hear. Rochester's refusal to imagine Jane as a social being in these stories is as childish as Jane's childhood rages and fantasies and as dangerous. Jane's subsequent refusal to play out his idea of her part is, among other things, a refusal to be a supporting character in a dubious—and irresponsible—tale of someone else's invention.

The most remarkable piece of evidence for the complexity of Brontë's interest in the issue of storytelling and truth is the single scene in which Jane herself becomes a set narrator within her own narration. This occurs on the eve of the interrupted wedding, when Jane tells Rochester the story of Bertha's nocturnal appearance in her room, and the tearing of the wedding veil. The scene represents so many tiers of stories within stories that it might almost stand for a miniature model of the novel as a whole. To begin with, the tale is elaborately set up as a ghost story: despite the fear and anguish which Bertha's visit would presumably have caused, Jane waits until the stroke of midnight to begin her tale and creates a shaped, suspenseful narrative by prefacing her account of Bertha's visit with two dream sequences. In them she fearfully imagines Rochester riding away into the romantic landscape (as he had ridden into it, in the earlier narrative), and sees a preliminary vision of the destroyed shell of Thornfield. In itself, this highly stylized and manipulated Gothic tale suggests several layers of confusion between fiction and lived experience, and between Jane's midnight tales and the tale of *Jane Eyre* she tells to us. The point of the scene is exactly that multiplication of confusion: it allows Rochester to maintain his hold over Jane's imagination by convincing her that Bertha's visit was "half dream, half reality." Jane's appearance as a Gothic narrator, so carefully "set" to emphasize the point, is clearly a dangerous position.

Even more fascinating is the way that, early in the scene, Jane talks about Rochester as though she were creating his character in her imagination:

> I smiled as I unfolded the wedding veil, and devised how I would teaze you about your aristocratic tastes, and your efforts to masque your plebeian bride in the attributes of a peeress. I thought how I would carry down to you the square of unembroidered blonde I had myself prepared as a covering for my low-born head, and ask if that was not good enough for a woman who could bring her husband neither fortune, beauty, nor connections. I saw plainly how you would look; and heard your impetuous republican answers, and your haughty disavowal of any necessity on your part to augment your wealth, or elevate your standing, by marrying either a purse or a coronet.

The overt point here is simply that Jane knows Rochester so well that she can imagine scenes between them, and her version of their relationship is certainly more accurate—to the "external" fiction—than are his stories about "mademoiselle on the moon." But this passage does two other things as well. It multiplies the layers of fiction-making again, showing Jane telling Rochester a story about making up scenes in which she invents his character, as though to say, "You are nothing more than a character in my fiction." It also introduces Jane's view of the story-pattern that she and Rochester belong to; it is the *Pamela* pattern of class fantasy: aristocrat marries dependent girl. Jane's discomfort with that story is clear enough in the dreams that follow, depicting abandonment and desolation. The position of dependency that the *Pamela* story implies will not do for her, and a good deal of the rest of the novel is designed to rewrite the scenario in her favor.

It is important throughout the scene that Jane thinks of the marriage as a way of dissolving into Rochester's life: "the life that lay before me—*your* life, sir—an existence so much more stirring and

expansive than my own." That Jane should present herself as a
Gothic tale-teller on the eve of a fraudulent wedding to Rochester's
"story" suggests that she is in the position of losing control of her
own story. Her flight from Rochester might thus be read as a search
for a true and equivalent story of her own.

When Jane leaves Thornfield to become the heroine of her own
life, her own story is conventional and fantastic enough. She sets
forth like any picaresque hero, loses her last shilling in the first scene,
discovers her true family, and inherits a fortune. The difference between this and Rochester's story is that it is not a romance, and that
Jane is the hero of it; now she is the one who appears at Moor House
with a story to conceal and a mystery to solve. That we are to experience all this as "story" is apparent when Brontë puts the tale of
Jane's inheritance into the mouth of St. John Rivers—not without
having him point out its conventionality: " 'I spoke of my impatience
to hear the sequel of a tale: on reflection, I find the matter will be
better managed by my assuming the narrator's part, and converting
you into a listener. Before commencing, it is but fair to warn you
that the story will sound somewhat hackneyed in your ears: but stale
details often regain a degree of freshness when they pass through
new lips.' " St. John suggests that a new teller might reanimate an
old tale, yet making Jane into an audience to her own story is another
of Brontë's distancing moves: no, even this is not the main story;
Jane is its passive heroine but not its narrator. The whole scene is
particularly delightful because Jane keeps interrupting with questions
about Rochester; in her version of her life he would clearly have to
be a major figure, while St. John chides her for forgetting "essential
points in pursuing trifles"; he would have her rejoice properly in her
role as missing heiress. In this way Brontë succeeds in using the
story-pattern of the inheritance plot to Jane's advantage, while refusing to allow us to think of Jane—or Jane to think of herself—as "that
kind of heroine."

When Jane leaves Moor House to find Rochester again, she does
not know what has happened to him and dreads knowing the outcome of his part of the plot. She finds out from yet another outside narrator, the "respectable-looking, middle-aged" host of "The
Rochester Arms." What has happened to Rochester attains in this
way the same "story" status as Jane's inheritance plot. Once again,
the metaphor is clearly worked: when Jane sees the burnt shell of
Thornfield, she responds as she did to the pictures of her youth:

"What story belonged to this disaster?"; now, of course, the pictures are scenes in her own life. Prepared for "a tale of misery," Jane's concern during the dialogue is to prevent the innkeeper from telling her part in the story. The scene is a funny counterpart to the one with St. John, for Jane wants to put Rochester into her story, but does her best to keep herself out of his.

But the host cannot and will not keep her out; his narrative insists that Jane is part of Rochester's story, moving back and forth from his eyewitness account of the "Gothic" fire to a more "moral" internal tale—the effect on Rochester of Jane's leaving. His version, fully sympathetic to Rochester, testifies to Jane's overwhelming power to affect Rochester's life: " 'a more spirited, bolder, keener gentleman than he was before that midge of a governess crossed him, you never saw, ma'am . . . for my part I have often wished that Miss Eyre had been sunk in the sea before she came to Thornfield Hall.' " He also describes Rochester as having become "savage" in self-imposed isolation—in the state of asocial imprisonment in overwhelmed feeling that Jane has worked against since the time of the red-room.

Like St. John's version of Jane's story, the innkeeper's tale does the work of setting Jane into a pattern without identifying her with it. Most dramatically, it makes Jane into the villain; she appears as the character who walked into Rochester's life, ruined it, and then rode off into the distance. We cannot, knowing Jane's internal experience, assent to this glimpse in a different mirror any more than Jane can. But even the inclusion of a suggestion—that her story could be read in quite another way that stresses Jane's responsibility for Rochester's pain—indicates Brontë's vigilant efforts to represent the choices in storytelling.

At the same time, the innkeeper's story prepares the way for Jane's return to be read as a mission of salvation: she alone, like the fairy-tale prince, can release Rochester from the prison of despair he has locked himself into. Since the novel has established that state of moral isolation as its most dangerous pole, Jane's return is thus defined not as another fall into fantastic and excessive feeling, but as a reasonable extrication from its extremes.

So Rochester's idea of Jane as his fairy-tale instrument of salvation comes true—but not until it has been rewritten in Jane's terms. Again, the peculiar dependent independence from conventional story-patterns comes up; by the end of the novel Jane has figured in so many different kinds of stories that it is difficult to characterize the novel in any one way. And that multiplicity may finally be the most important point. It is not enough to say that Brontë reanimated the Gothic, or that *Jane Eyre* takes its place among patterns established by fairy tales or "governess novels," though these arguments are important contributions to an appreciation of Brontë's art. For at every turn the novel is conscious of its status among fictions, and of the difficulty of describing personal history in any way that does not turn it into one pattern or another. The many kinds of stories that are explicitly brought up in the text are there partly to be used, partly to be exorcised and denied as limitations in the scope of Jane's character or Brontë's narrative powers. In the end it becomes impossible to answer the question "Then what kind of story is Jane's life?" For it is the life of a storyteller in a world full of fictions, a teller whose claim to originality as a character rests in her ability to take charge of so many kinds of stories in a narrative that seems both to credit and to quarrel with them all.

Dreaming of Children: Literalization in *Jane Eyre*

Margaret Homans

"There was no possibility of taking a walk that day. . . . I was glad of it. I never liked long walks, especially on chilly afternoons." With this opening assertion, Charlotte Brontë founds her novel on her heroine's skepticism about the experiences in nature that her sister's just-completed novel so ambiguously celebrates. In reading *Wuthering Heights,* and in considering Dorothy Wordsworth's journals [in *Bearing the Word*], we have been looking primarily at a range of responses to the potential identification between women writers and a female or maternal presence in nature. Dorothy Wordsworth embraces a sympathetic identification with what her brother identifies as female in nature and organizes her writing to protect nature from the law of the symbolic language that he practices. While Emily Brontë shares Dorothy Wordsworth's interests, she also shares the poet's. *Wuthering Heights* celebrates Cathy's resistance to symbolic systems and to the father's law, celebrating her return to childhood that is a return to nature. At the same time, the novel suggests that nature, identified with literal meaning, threatens the writing of fiction as much as Cathy's regressive love of nature threatens her life. Despite Jane's dislike for taking walks, parts of *Jane Eyre* take place in the landscape of *Wuthering Heights*—the Yorkshire moors—but to different effect. Each novelist transforms the moors into a symbolic system, but while Emily Brontë undertakes this project ambivalently, her sister accepts it far more wholeheartedly. Charlotte shares

From *Bearing the Word: Language and Female Experience in Nineteenth-Century Women's Writing.* © 1986 by the University of Chicago. University of Chicago Press, 1986.

her sister's attraction to a nonlinguistic literal, but she shares to a much greater degree her sister's awareness that this attraction contradicts the aims of the novelist.

As we have seen, the literal is historically associated with nature, and especially in and just after the Romantic period, it is against identification with nature that women writers stage their ambivalent defenses against becoming identified with the literal and the object. Projected onto women by masculine texts, internalized and reproduced by women writers, an identification of the mother with nature might seem to offer women access to power, since, taking the form of nature, the literal is the final, maternal object of desire. Yet because the desired object is also so feared by androcentric culture, to accept that identification might be to stop writing and speaking intelligibly within the symbolic order. Both Charlotte and Emily Brontë figure this silence as death, because the mother's place in the symbolic order is to be absent. While *Wuthering Heights* entertains the possibility that the mother's place also has power and value of its own, *Jane Eyre* entertains only in order to defend against it the seductive possibility of a woman's becoming the literal.

Wuthering Heights dramatizes the dangers and attractions, not only of a woman writer's identification with a feminized and literal nature, but also specifically of the role in this process of maternity and of a mother's reproduction in her daughter of her own childhood. In keeping with the novel's ambivalence about women's relation to the law, Cathy's childbirth is both contained within the law of patriliny and outside the law. She gives birth simultaneously to the heir of the Lintons and to the wild and ghostly child-self who haunts Lockwood at the start of the novel, the outlaw, antithetical to everything Lockwood stands for, whose wrist he rubs on the broken window pane "till the blood ran down and soaked the bed-clothes." This [essay] will extend our inquiry about maternity to a reading of *Jane Eyre,* in the context of investigating Charlotte Brontë's relation to the literal. Like *Wuthering Heights, Jane Eyre* reveals its author's knowledge both that motherhood is implicated in women's culturally imposed identification with the literal and that, as a reproduction of the literal, it models a kind of writing that endangers a text's place within what we are calling the symbolic order. But in keeping with its own greater acceptance of the law, *Jane Eyre* does not share the sense of liberating possibility with which Emily Brontë endows her representation of childbirth.

Jane Eyre presents the fear of the objectification of the self in a variety of ways that make particularly explicit the connection between femininity and objectification. Jane fears that Rochester objectifies her when he wants to dress her in jewels and silks that correspond, not to her individual character, but to his abstract idea of Mrs. Edward Fairfax Rochester. Like Cathy shocked by the alienness of her mirror image, Jane is shocked twice by what she sees in the mirror, in the red-room when "the strange little figure there gazing at [her] had the effect of a real spirit," and again on the morning of her wedding, when the mirror's "robed and veiled figure, so unlike [her] usual self that it seemed almost the image of a stranger" represents both the appeal and the threat of having her subjectivity replaced by a beautiful object. This [essay], however, will examine the novel's exploration of the feminine temptation to become an object through two kinds of literalization: the circumstances of childbearing and the Gothic literalization of subjective states with which, in the novel, childbearing is often inauspiciously associated. (To draw on an already familiar example from *Wuthering Heights,* which makes a similar association, in Lockwood's "dream" Brontë pairs the apparition of a ghost with what we later learn is the birth of Cathy's child-self.) In both the Gothic and in childbirth, what was once internal acquires its own objective reality; and in both situations, the heroine is in a position to become identified with the object world on which her subjectivity is projected.

As Charlotte and Emily Brontë write it, the Gothic both acknowledges and protests the place to which women are relegated in romantic myths of subjectivity and transcendence. In Gothic novels generally, subjective states are so fully and literally projected into a social framework as to alter physical reality. Specifically, the Gothic literalizes the romantic imagination, and it is this literalization that produces its terror. When Heathcliff at the end of his life sees Cathy "in every cloud, in every tree—filling the air at night, and caught by glimpses in every object by day" (chap. 33), the effective projection of his desire literalizes Coleridge's figure for the way the imagination shapes the perceptual world, the "fair luminous cloud / Enveloping the Earth" ("Dejection: An Ode," 11.54–55). This pattern of literalization operates in all Gothic works, but it has special implications for women, which the Brontës make explicit. The romantic imagination that the Gothic literalizes is predominantly a masculine mode: Coleridge defines the imagination so that the poet is the patrilineal inheritor of a distinctly masculine God's self-assertion "I AM." Just as Mr. Ramsay's metaphysical speculations depend upon and produce a feminine "phantom kitchen table" for the puzzled Lily Briscoe, the desiring romantic imagination assumes feminine phantoms of desire. And just as Lily impertinently imagines the table back into existence, the Brontës' female Gothic literalizes Romanticism's phantoms.

The difficulty, especially as far as Charlotte Brontë is concerned, is that literalization is precisely what female figures embody in romantic myth. A woman writer's practice of literalization, like Lily's, would seem to be a protest against romantic speculation; yet in a larger sense, that protest has already been scripted within what it protests. But if the Brontës' Gothic rehearses women's fate within the symbolic order, at least it does so self-consciously and therefore skeptically. (Although both Charlotte and Emily Brontë use Gothic elements in their novels, and although the structure of Gothic literalization is essentially the same in *Wuthering Heights* and *Jane Eyre,* *Jane Eyre* is more skeptical than *Wuthering Heights* about Gothic literalization and about its implications for women, for Emily envisages the possibility of reclaiming the literal and literalization for an original female power in a way that Charlotte does not.) It may be that the Gothic became historically a predominantly female mode because it lends itself so well to women writers' responses to the cultural identification of "woman" with the literal. It could be that Charlotte Brontë uses the Gothic, where all sorts of literalizations occur, not because she is incapable of what her culture would define as a liberating transcendence of the body, but rather because it enables her to criticize the double position in which culture places her. To the extent that a woman writes within what we have retrospectively described as the symbolic order, she accepts cultural definitions of femininity, yet those definitions situate her as a woman outside the symbolic. Because as a woman she has been excluded from the symbolic order, as a writer she feels she must continually confront and defend against that exclusion. While Woolf can celebrate Lily's literalizing imagination (in part because she also imagines other things for her woman artist to do), Charlotte Brontë uses the Gothic with ambivalence and uses her ambivalence to protest the objectification of the feminine that the Gothic enacts.

We can see this ambivalence at work in the way *Jane Eyre* frequently entertains Gothic possibilities, then appears to undermine them with rational explanations, and still later undermines those rational explanations themselves. Ultimately, as we will see, in a final twist, Brontë undermines even that return to Gothic literalization. The most familiar example of this pattern is Jane's chastisement both of herself and of her reader when she finds herself wondering about the demonic laughter that issues from Grace Poole's attic room. "Sometimes I saw her; she would . . . go down to the kitchen, and shortly return, generally (oh, romantic reader, forgive me for telling the plain truth!) bearing a pot of porter. Her appearance always acted as a damper to the curiosity raised by her oral oddities" (chap. 12). But the laugh in the attic is only temporarily explained away. Jane errs in denying the Gothic's literalization of speculation. That the source of those "oral oddities" has an existence and a history more horrifying than the wildest fantasy demonstrates that her allegiance to "the plain truth" offers no escape from the dangers of subjectivity, for it is precisely in the realm of "the plain truth" that Jane's fears and subversive wishes take their most terrifying form. In Brontë's Gothic, terror originates in the heroine's confinement to the world of objects.

This reading is confirmed by Brontë's curious and unconventional emphasis on Jane's fear of any apparition, whether good or bad. Apparitions horrify, not because they are evil, but because they appear at all. This is the case in Jane and Rochester's supernatural long-distance conversation at the end of the novel, but more strikingly in the novel's first Gothic instance, the apparition of Mr. Reed in the red-room. Thinking of stories about spirits returning to earth to avenge the oppressed, Jane relates, "I wiped my tears and hushed my sobs, fearful lest any sign of violent grief might waken a preternatural voice to comfort me, or elicit from the gloom some haloed face, bending over me with strange pity. This idea, consolatory in theory, I felt would be terrible if realised" (chap. 2). This separation of "theory" and "realization" allows Jane to establish that, for this text, any passage from subjective to objective, or from internal to external, is potentially terrifying. The introduction of these terms widens the implications of the use of the Gothic and connects them explicitly to the larger issue of women's identification with the literal.

The Gothic's literalization of imaginative or other subjective states often coincides with representations of a rather different kind of literalization, the experience or idea of childbirth. That women bear children and men do not is the simple origin of this complex and troubling tradition that associates women with the literal and with nature, an association that at once appeals to and repels women writers. Both novels foreground a curious connection between their most Gothic elements and motherhood. The transitory experience of being a mother is the central and recurring metaphor for the abundant sense of danger in *Jane Eyre* (just as the plot of *Wuthering Heights* turns on the main character's death in childbirth and her subsequent transformation into a ghost). The specific connection between the literalization of subjective states and childbirth's actual passage from internal to external takes place in dreams about children. Like other internal states in the Gothic mode, dreams are literalized in the object world, and the ambiguous process of their literalization mirrors and reinforces an ambivalence that is almost always integral to the imagery of childbearing in the two novels.

Neither Charlotte nor Emily Brontë was, at the time of writing, in a position to experience or even to anticipate actual motherhood, but my concern here is with a view of the subject of production that might more likely (though not necessarily) be shared by women than by men. Any literary woman of the nineteenth century would have assumed that marriage and motherhood would end her career. Further, the thought of the event of childbirth itself would have had highly ambiguous connotations for any pre-twentieth-century woman. In the nineteenth century, giving birth was not unlikely to be fatal to the mother or to the child or to both, and to fear childbirth or associate it with death would have been quite reasonable. (The Brontës' mother died when they were young children, probably of complications resulting from bearing six children in seven years. . . . Although Mrs. Brontë's death may well have left her daughters with a powerful nostalgia for mothering, a nostalgia that can be traced in what is known of Charlotte's life, the response to the mother's death within the literary text is an overriding drive to dissociate the writing self from the idea of the mother because of the various threats she poses to writing.) The commonplaceness of the dangers of childbirth is reflected in its casual treatment in Romantic and other nineteenth-century fiction, where a mother's death in childbirth is often merely a convention for producing an interesting protagonist. Women who become mothers in novels tend to die psychically if they do not die literally; survivors usually subordinate their identities to those of their husbands or of their marriageable daughters. Within the conventions of fiction, childbirth puts an end to the mother's existence as an individual. And we have seen [elsewhere] how a poetic myth of language such as Wordsworth's in *The Prelude* likewise requires the death or absence of the mother.

This negative reading of childbearing is echoed in more recent psychoanalytic accounts that may be suggestive for the nineteenth century. Writing in 1945, Helene Deutsch describes the persistence of fears of childbirth despite medical advances in the last half of the nineteenth century that reduced childbirth mortality "to a minimum." She argues that the fear of actual death had all along been a screen for an expression of psychic fears, particularly of separation. That the unborn child both has and lacks its own identity complicates a pregnant woman's identity. The boundary between her identity and that of the child within her is quite literally permeable, psychically and physically. Her own sense of identity is quite naturally called into question: before birth there is an other, perhaps sensed as parasitical, resident within the self, while after birth a part of the self is gone. Fear of losing a part of the body's content is part of the separation fear, "but it is only one component, among others, of a general fear of separation from the child conceived as a part of the woman's own ego, a fear that assumes the character of the fear of death." This fear of loss of self, Deutsch argues, is augmented by a feeling of powerlessness in relation to the process that has been set in motion: "Whether she wants to or not, she who has created this new life must obey its power; its rule is expected, yet invisible, implacable. Because of these very qualities it necessarily produces fear."

To say that the mother projects into the object world something that was once internal and that now has its own independent existence, and that that projection may produce fear, is also to describe the structure of the Gothic (notice how Gothic Deutsch's language is). Childbirth, thus construed, almost too vividly figures the Gothic pattern in which unconscious projection takes actual form. What the male romantic mind does figuratively, the womb can do literally, and literal self-duplication invites the fear that what one has created will subsequently overpower and eradicate the self.

Jane Eyre establishes a complex series of connectives between danger or trouble and figures of childbirth or of mother-child relationships, comprising the prophetic dreams of children and also the narrative use of such figuration. This series originates in Jane's recollection of Bessie's folk belief that "to dream of children was a sure sign of trouble, either to one's self or to one's kin" (chap. 21), and both Bessie's experience and Jane's verify the belief. Initially the dream self is Jane, and the child and the trouble it portends are quite external to her, but in successive dreams the sense of self is divided, confusingly, between child and parent figures, or it shifts altogether from parent to child. Introducing this idea, Jane says that "scarcely a night" for a week had passed "that had not brought with it a dream of an infant: which I sometimes hushed in my arms, sometimes dandled on my knee, sometimes watched playing with daisies on a lawn. . . . It was a wailing child this night, and a laughing one the next: now it nestled close to me, and now it ran from me. . . . It was from companionship with this baby-phantom I had been roused on that moonlight night" (chap. 21) by the "trouble" of Mason's outcry at Bertha's attack. Here Jane is clearly distinct from the child, and the trouble external to her. But it is also following this series of dreams that she is called to the sickbed of Mrs. Reed, who deliriously dreams aloud of Jane as a troublesome child: "I have had more trouble with that child than any one would believe. Such a burden to be left on my hands" (chap. 21). Mrs. Reed wished that Jane would die of the fever at Lowood; she hated Jane as a baby "the first time I set my eyes on it—a sickly, whining, pining thing! It would wail in its cradle all night long." From her dream of self as adult and other as child, Jane now becomes the child and the other in someone else's subjective experience. Splitting the sense of self between child and adult, these dreams question and break down the boundary between subject and object, between self and other.

Following this dream inversion of self and other, childbirth enters the figurative structure of the novel as a way of describing the danger that the self will become something other than itself. Returning from Gateshead, fearfully certain that Rochester will marry Blanche Ingram, Jane describes her feelings thus: "And then I strangled a new-born agony—a deformed thing which I could not persuade myself to own and rear—and ran on" (chap. 22). This new-born agony has a twin sister, another of Jane's metaphoric offspring, who at first does not appear to be either as undesirable or as threatening. The morning after her engagement Jane has a feeling of "almost fear" on hearing herself addressed as Jane Rochester, and the night before the wedding she still senses and fears this radical split between her single and married selves. By the next day, she says, she will be on the road to London, "or rather, not I, but one Jane Rochester, a person whom as yet I knew not," and whose name she refuses to affix to her trunks:

> Mrs. Rochester! She did not exist: she would not be born till to-morrow, some time after eight o'clock A.M.; and I would wait to be assured she had come into the world alive before I assigned to her all that property. It was enough that in yonder closet, opposite my dressing-table, garments said to be hers had already displaced my black stuff Lowood frock and straw bonnet: for not to me appertained that suit of wedding raiment.
>
> (chap. 25)

Like Bessie's prophetic dreams of children, this metaphor of a child prophecies danger. As Mrs. Rochester's clothes displace Jane's, so does Jane fear that her desire to love and be the object of love will entirely displace her equally strong wish to maintain her independence. The birth metaphor employed here should not necessarily suggest displacement, as the exchange of one name for another so neatly does; yet apparently for Brontë the image of childbirth connotes primarily loss of self. Jane Eyre will have to die in giving birth to Mrs. Rochester. Especially because the change of a married woman's name is determined by law, the situation corresponds to the aspect of Cathy's childbirth that is within the law, her production of a patrilineal heir who makes her own existence unnecessary. The "trouble" with which all the novel's dreamt and figurative children are associated may originate in this vision of motherhood in which the mother vanishes as the child is born.

Although in fictive time, Jane's two best-known dream children precede her vision of Mrs. Rochester as an unborn child, she narrates these events in reverse order, so that any reading of her dreams is colored by the passage about Mrs. Rochester. In these dreams, Jane is the surrogate mother of a child she seems not to know, but that they almost directly follow an image of birth suggests that the child does belong to the dreamer, who is unwilling to acknowledge it. In the first dream, the dreamer is traveling an unknown road, in the rain and dark, "burdened with the charge of a little child: a very small creature, too young and feeble to walk, and which shivered in my cold arms and wailed piteously in my ear" (chap. 25). Thinking that Rochester is ahead on the road, the dreamer strains to overtake or call to him, "but my movements were fettered" and Rochester vanishes. In the second dream, developing out of the first, Thorn-field is a ruin through which the dreamer wanders. "I thought that of all the stately front nothing remained but a shell-like wall, very high, and very fragile-looking. . . . I still carried the unknown little child: I might not lay it down anywhere, however tired were my arms—however much its weight impeded my progress, I must re-tain it" (chap. 25). Hearing Rochester galloping away in the distance, she climbs the thin wall, frantic for one last glimpse of him; as the wall gives way beneath her, "the child clung round my neck in terror, and almost strangled me." She reaches the windy summit only to see Rochester vanishing, and dreamer and child fall as the wall crumbles. The dream child clearly represents some aspect of Jane's life, but what that might be is not clear. The child may be "Mrs. Rochester," the new self to which Jane pictures herself fatally giving birth at the moment of her marriage; it may be Jane's love for Rochester; it may also represent Jane's own neglected childhood, as suggested by the close parallel with Mrs. Reed's description of Jane as a burdensome and wailing infant; the "new-born agony" that Jane "strangles" may also be present here. However we interpret the child, what is signif-icant is that subjectivity is divided between the dream-self and the dream-child. That there are several equally plausible readings sug-gests that what generates the sense of danger is not the particular part of the self the child represents, but that such a representation or division of the self into parts occurs at all. The dreams give Jane an intimation of what it would be like to become other than herself.

These two dreams in which Jane figures as the unwilling mother surrogate for a difficult child-self are complemented two nights later by a third dream in which the child is Jane and the mother is a benign spirit. The threat presented in the first two dreams seems to have been at once fulfilled and avoided. The self has become a child, yet the wedding has failed to take place, and the dream child now is manifestly not Mrs. Rochester. Unable and unwilling to give birth to that troublesome child, Jane regresses to a version of her own childhood. She dreams that she is back at Gateshead, lying in the red-room and watching the same ghostly light that once terrified her, but now the ceiling resolves into clouds and that light into moonlight and then into the visionary mother:

> She broke forth as never moon yet burst from cloud: a
> hand first penetrated the sable folds and waved them away;

then, not a moon, but a white human form shone in the azure, inclining a glorious brow earthward. It gazed and gazed and gazed on me. It spoke to my spirit: immeasurably distant was the tone, yet so near, it whispered in my heart—

"My daughter, flee temptation!"

"Mother, I will."

(chap. 27)

This dream of being the child of a loving and protective mother makes an ambiguous conclusion to the sequence of dreams and figures of children, since so far no child—real, figurative, or dreamt—has given or received anything but trouble. Although the dreamer rejoices, this dream must logically represent the fulfillment of the threat of the previous dreams, with the suggestion that the dream deceives as it soothes.

These dreams of children represent Jane's unconscious investigation of the state of becoming other than herself or of deferring altogether to projections, and the process of this investigation is repeated in the literalization or coming true of the dreams that characterizes the Gothic pattern. All the dreams come true in some way, but from one dream to the next they come true in increasingly literal ways. To be prophetic of trouble, according to Bessie's superstition, the dream need only include the apparently arbitrary symbol of the child, and in the original series of dreams that brought out Jane's recollection of Bessie's story, the child represents danger whether it laughs or cries. But in the pair of dreams preceding the wedding, both child and mother are themselves vividly in trouble, so that the dreamt child is not simply an arbitrary symbol but a metaphor. That the dream child appears to represent some feature of Jane's life (and that Rochester riding away from Jane in the dream prefigures their separation three days later) suggests that the child as metaphor would match only Jane's particular situation. (If the passage from symbol to metaphor moves in the direction of relative literalization, the sequence is finally completed much later on [though not with reference to the mother and child figure that concerns us here] by the uncanny literal repetition of Jane's vision in the object world. The shell-like battlements that she climbs in the second dream, burdened with the child, are precisely realized in Thornfield's ruin by fire. Typical of *Jane Eyre*'s handling of the Gothic, when the dream picture of

Thornfield comes true so literally, Jane very casually relegates to a subordinate clause her acknowledgment of the uncanniness of the situation, as if the Gothic's turn from visionary fear to the world of substance were a demystification, and not a further mystery: "The front was, as I had once seen it in a dream, but a shell-like wall, very high and very fragile looking.") Dreams also literalize each other: just as the second of the pair of dreams extends the action and implications of the first, the third dream, in which Jane explicitly dreams of herself as the child, realizes the unpleasant implication of the first two dreams, that Jane is herself the child as well as the mother. Looking further back, the third dream also appears to spell out and explain the morally ambiguous ghost that confused Jane as a child in the red-room. Set in the same scene, the more recent vision soothes where Mr. Reed terrified; but the vision of the shining human form "inclining a glorious brow earthward" and speaking words of comfort literalizes what the child had only imagined to be the ultimate terror. Her fear then was that her grief would "waken a preternatural voice to comfort me, or elicit from the gloom some haloed face, bending over me with strange pity," and that is exactly what happens in the dream. The passage from "theory" to "realization" was what was "terrible" in the red-room, and the same turns out to be true here, in the passage from the dream to the next few days' actual experience. Jane finds the dream's figures enacted in the object world, and like other literalizations, these threaten her life.

In the waking scenes of flight and wandering that directly follow, the prophetic dream comes true in the literalization of the dreamt mother: "I have no relative but the universal mother, Nature: I will seek her breast and ask repose" (chap. 28). Mother Nature is a mother only figuratively, yet because Jane names the landscape in this way and insists on and extends the figure, the dreamt mother must be connected to this very tangible one. Naming nature "mother," Jane accepts the tradition that identifies the feminine with the object world, an identification that at this point seems very appealing. The visionary mother encouraged Jane to flee temptation, and when Jane wanders into nature after leaving Rochester, the landscape appears maternal because it appears to help on her flight from temptation. This positive view of nature may represent what Nancy Chodorow would identify as the daughter's continued close connection to her mother long past her entry into androcentric culture, a connection that, however, a daughter who is a figure for the novelist, whose main allegiance is to the father's symbol making, finds very difficult to sustain and finally rejects.

As on every other occasion, the coming true of a dream, the discovery in the object world of what was at one time purely subjective, is actually more frightening than the subjective experience itself, even though Jane's tone at first directs us to find it consoling. Mother Nature betrays her daughter, but to be her daughter is dangerous enough, and betrayal is inherent in the relation. In the dream, Jane shifts her identity from adult to child without making the concomitant change from self to other that previous dreams intimated, and being this somewhat regressive child-self is clearly preferable to the loss of self that giving birth to Mrs. Rochester would have represented. It appears now that the transformation of self into other was only deferred: simultaneous with the literalization of her dream, Jane as a child of Mother Nature finds herself in the position of being identified with the literal, first deceived into seeking this identification, then almost forced into it. This experience's close connection with all of the dreams, where Jane has been a mother as well as a child, also suggests an identity between Jane and the mother figure herself, as a continuation of that perpetual shifting between subject and object that the dreams introduce. Either way, being like nature or being nature's child, the danger is the same identification with the literal that jeopardizes both Jane's sense of self and her life.

Just before making this reference to Mother Nature, Jane describes her surroundings. Whitcross, where she alights after her destinationless coach ride away from Thornfield, appropriately signals her entry into a land of literalized dreams, because the name's meaning is as close to literal as any naming can be. Whitcross is not the name of a town but of a whitewashed stone pillar with four arms: a white cross. Like Dorothy Wordsworth's self-naming refuges, Whitcross names only itself. Yet whereas Dorothy Wordsworth's resistance to the symbolic order makes such a discovery fortuitous, Jane's allegiance to that order makes this discovery signal disaster. Jane has neither money, the symbol of symbols, nor any tie to human society, and lacking either a speakable past or an imaginable future, she has, like the self-referential Whitcross, no significance. (Of course, to say that the white cross, or Jane's lack of money, figures Jane's reduced state, and to remember that while the white cross may not signify a town it does signify in a different way by pointing to four destinations, is already to acknowledge that literal meaning is never quite representable, yet this is as close as a written text can come to literality.) "Strangers would wonder what I am doing, lingering here at the sign–post, evidently objectless and lost. I might be questioned: I could give no answer but what would sound incredible and excite suspicion" (chap. 28). That she describes her situation in terms of a lack of language explicitly names Jane's experience as literal. To be "objectless" is to cease being a subject. That this passage concerning Jane's reduction to her physical being concludes with the reminder that matter is traditionally female deepens the danger of her position and defines that danger as a particularly feminine one.

Setting out from Whitcross, Jane arrives at a protective place in the heath, a soft hollow sheltered by high banks. As night very gently falls, "Nature seemed to me benign and good; I thought she loved me, outcast as I was; and I, who from man could anticipate only mistrust, rejection, insult, clung to her with filial fondness. To-night, at least, I would be her guest—as I was her child: my mother would lodge me without money and without price" (chap. 28). The curious phrasing of the last sentence here suggests Jane's insight that she is not truly nature's child, but only nature's nonpaying guest. That the passage proposes various images for nature (mother, innkeeper) creates a consciousness of figuration that serves to defend against, while the passage otherwise appears to endorse, the possibility that Jane is nature's child. Even more striking is the doubt implicit in "Nature seemed to me benign and good; I thought she loved me." This doubt is confirmed the next morning when the evening's relative comfort gives way to pressing exhaustion and hunger. Jane no longer refers to the landscape as a mother, the mother having abandoned the child who may have been deluded in imagining herself protected. In becoming actual, what seemed benign as a vision becomes neglectful, even malignant.

Jane discovers here on the moor, as does the dying Cathy in *Wuthering Heights,* that to become part of nature is to die. The solace nature offers is not just an illusion concealing death; that solace is itself death:

> What a still, hot, perfect day! What a golden desert this spreading moor! Everywhere sunshine. I wished I could live in it and on it. I saw a lizard run over the crag; I saw a bee busy among the sweet bilberries. I would fain at the moment have become bee or lizard, that I might have found fitting nutriment, permanent shelter here. . . .

> Hopeless of the future, I wished but this—that my Maker had that night thought good to require my soul of me while I slept; and that this weary frame, absolved by death from further conflict with fate, had now but to decay quietly, and mingle in peace with the soil of this wilderness.
>
> (chap. 28)

Jane's wish to "live in it and on it" echoes Cathy's dying wish to be "really with it, and in it" (chap. 15). That Cathy's "it" refers at once to nature and to a transcendent realm beyond death suggests that Jane's "it," which seems to refer here only to the moor, will soon refer also to the world into which Cathy dies. That there is at this point almost no difference between Mother Nature and her daughter almost completes the dreams' efforts to blur the distinctions between mother and child, subject and object. In the context of the dreams, to become the child is to become an object, while to become part of this mother would also be to turn into an object.

Jane resists the fate that Cathy embraces because she retains her consciousness of difference: she knows that to identify and mingle with nature necessitates dying. Breaking into the middle of this passage, interrupting that tempting continuity, is Jane's recollection that she is not a child of nature but "a human being, and had a human being's wants: I must not linger where there was nothing to supply them." The true child of Mother Nature, one that finds "permanent shelter" in her breast, is the lizard or the bee, never the living woman. Jane's wish that she had died in the night and the temptation as she walks to stop and "submit resistlessly to the apathy that clogged heart and limb" represent nature's residual pressure and conflict with "life, . . . with all its requirements, and pains, and responsibilities," which prevents Jane from yielding. Nature is now a dangerous tempter, in contrast to that mother within Jane's mind who told Jane to "flee temptation." She returns to her starting point at Whitcross, to begin again; soon she is again on the verge of giving in to nature's temptation when she is recalled to consciousness by the chime of a church bell and then by the sight of a village and cultivated fields that, by representing human life, help her resist the literality of the wild moor.

If nature is no longer the mother and Jane no longer the child, she can resist nature's appeal that she become part of the literal. Toward the end of the second day of her wanderings, Jane, having undergone extreme humiliation and physical suffering, finds that she has "once more drawn near the tract of moorland" (chap. 28). In the same location, she seeks a version of the first evening's repose, but here the consciousness of her difference sustains her in her disillusionment with the dream vision's promises. She calls on Providence to guide her, not on Mother Nature to soothe her. Recognizing that she may die, she prefers a death in nature to "a workhouse coffin . . . in a pauper's grave." But in place of her earlier sympathetic identification with nature and her subsequent wish to "mingle in peace with the soil of this wilderness," Jane now images a death in nature as a violent separation from the soil: crows and ravens will pick the flesh from her bones. As if in response to her state of mind, nature now repudiates Jane. Having passed beyond

> a few fields, almost as wild and unproductive as the heath
> from which they were scarcely reclaimed, . . . it remained
> now only to find a hollow where I could lie down, and feel
> at least hidden, if not secure: but all the surface of the
> waste looked level. It showed no variation but of tint;
> green, where rush and moss overgrew the marshes; black,
> where the dry soil bore only heath. Dark as it was getting,
> I could still see these changes; though but as mere alterna-
> tions of light and shade: for colour had faded with the
> daylight.
>
> (chap. 28)

Difference is necessary for human signification, and this wild, unvarying sterility represents nature's closure to such meaning. Nature is more than fatal here; it is unwilling to help Jane in any project, even her death. In the earlier "golden desert" vision of this same fatal moorland, in which Jane briefly envies the bee and the lizard, it turns out that nature's vitality was an illusion produced by light, hiding the moor's true barrenness. This last picture of the moorland completes the literalization of the original maternal vision, the metaphor still adhering in "the dry soil bore only heath." This landscape's life-threatening sameness makes it the extreme form of all the novel's literalizations, wherever figural structure gives way to actuality. All literalizations here tend toward death. (Readers using the Penguin edition find this point made even more strongly by a misprint: "black, where the dry soil bore only death." There is no authority for this reading in any of the editions supervised by the author.)

Jane survives this confrontation with the fatally literal by means of various kinds of figuration that protect her from psychic and physical death. Directly after her vision of the undifferentiated landscape, the plot offers her a chance of life, a turn of events that appears to be not only paralleled but actually generated by a rhetorical turn from almost literal naming to dense figuration: "My eye still roved over the sullen swell, and along the moor edge, vanishing amidst the wild scenery; when at one dim point, far in among the marshes and ridges, a light sprang up" (chap. 28). This light returns the reader to the complex world of multiple signification that imparts textual life where literal meaning denies it. Cautious now of illusions, Jane at first thinks it is an "*ignis fatuus*"; but what is important about her effort to interpret this sight is that she speculates at such length. If it is not an illusion, it may be a bonfire. When it remains steady, she decides it is a candle in a window, but she subjects even that interpretation to further interpretation. Like Emily Brontë's Lockwood, who cures his flu by substituting tame metaphors for wild moors, Jane rescues herself by making nature into figures. The candle next becomes "my star" of "hope"; finally it repeats an image from one of Jane's visionary paintings, subordinating the actual landscape to a wholly different and entirely internal realm of psychic signification. It is as if, appropriately, Jane were saved by her ability to create figures. Painting herself back into life, she reverses the process of literalization.

From the vantage point of this reading of *Jane Eyre,* I wish to return briefly to *Wuthering Heights* to clarify, by contrasting the two novels, my reading of their structures of literalization and figuration and of their thematics of childbirth. Much as Jane's dreams of herself as child come true in the form of her subjection to nature, Cathy dreams herself as a child, and that dream comes true in the form of the child to which she regresses and later in the form of the ghostly child-self who appears to Lockwood. (Indeed, Lockwood's "dream" of Cathy is itself prophetic in something of the same way that dreams of children are in *Jane Eyre.* It "comes true" in the Gothic sense that Heathcliff knows the objective reality of what Lockwood takes to be "imagination," and in the literary sense that it prefigures the novel's actual violence, its scenes of exiled wanderers, and its orphans.) But Cathy seeks what Jane actively resists: a merging with nature that is also a return to childhood and that is, incidentally for Cathy but crucially for Jane, also death. Jane reverses the process of literalization embodied in the coming true of her dreams, and she resists altogether the literalization embodied in childbirth, while Cathy embraces both.

Jane's almost becoming part of the fatally literal in nature began with her unwillingness to give birth to Mrs. Rochester. When Jane Eyre contemplates giving metaphorical birth to Mrs. Rochester, she justifiably fears that the law will cause the "child" to replace and supersede the "mother." This is exactly what happens to Cathy, when her reproduction of an heir for the Lintons makes her own identity unnecessary within the law. Because childbirth is defined in *Jane Eyre* as entirely within the law, its only meaning is the mother's self-replacement and death. The novel does not acknowledge the ex-tralegal definition of motherhood that in *Wuthering Heights* makes Cathy's reproduction of her child-self a happy restoration. For Cathy, in giving birth, also remains partly outside the law, as we have seen, reproducing the lawless childhood self that she yearns to become again. Similarly, Jane temporarily regresses from being a mother figure to being a child, though for her this occurs through refusing to "give birth" in a way that would perpetuate and subor-dinate her to the law. Like Cathy (and even more explicitly), Jane becomes a child of Mother Nature; but again because it has no place for the outlaw, the novel presents this return to childhood and the death it would bring with it in nothing like the positive terms of *Wuthering Heights*. The stories of the two heroines, then, because they make different assumptions about the structure and the mean-ing of childbirth as a form of literalization, conclude in different con-sequences: while Cathy's production of a child fulfills her desire to be permanently a child, Jane's failure to give birth to her figurative child allows her to survive and grow. In both cases, the potential of motherhood is a transformation of the self or subjectivity into a lit-eral object, a transformation that Cathy desires and Jane at first courts but finally refuses. While Jane comes to understand the danger that to become the child of her dreams would be to merge with objective nature and to transfer the self from subject to object, the view of the same transference expressed by Cathy's situation is al-most wholly positive.

The threat that Charlotte Brontë has Mother Nature pose to Jane's identity and existence expresses her sense of the danger to all women of the identification of nature as mother. The temptation to become part of a feminized nature, to become a feminized object like nature, amounts in Brontë's view to a temptation to die, for it would be to join the dead mother, to accept exclusion from what her culture defines as human. By a curiously defensive logic, because Mother Nature is already dead, she might kill the writer who is a daughter, so the writer must kill Mother Nature first. Both Emily and Charlotte Brontë see that a woman, a mother, has been buried in the landscape of Romanticism, and both know they have been complicitous in placing her there yet again. In order to assert her allegiance to her culture's dominant myth of language, Charlotte Brontë dramatizes the near-murder of a woman at the hand of Mother Nature. Like Lockwood's snowstorm, this threat justifies Jane's subsequent betrayal of nature. The writer must betray the mother. Emily Brontë may protest this murder by bringing the mother to life again, but she does so only briefly, and only from the perspective of a mad and dying mother. Although the first Cathy in *Wuthering Heights* would view Jane's behavior as a betrayal of Mother Nature, Emily Brontë's view is not wholly contained in the story of the first Cathy. Just as Jane, having almost identified herself with nature's otherness, leaves it by multiplying significations and by thinking of her own figurative art, *Wuthering Heights* continues past Cathy's death to offer a daughter's history more in keeping with the rules of law. Like the story of the second Cathy in relation to the first, Charlotte Brontë offers a correction of a prior story, a story in which the attractions of the mother's place were even more adventurously explored.

Chronology

1812   The Reverend Patrick Brontë marries Maria Branwell.
1814   Maria Brontë, their first child, born.
1815   Elizabeth Brontë born.
1816   Charlotte Brontë born on April 21.
1817   Patrick Branwell Brontë, the only son, born in June.
1818   Emily Jane Brontë born on July 30.
1820   Anne Brontë born on January 17. The Brontë family moves to the parsonage at Haworth, near Bradford, Yorkshire.
1821   Mrs. Brontë dies of cancer in September. Her sister, Elizabeth Branwell, takes charge of the household.
1824   Maria and Elizabeth attend the Clergy Daughters' School at Cowan Bridge. Charlotte follows them in August, and Emily in November.
1825   The two oldest girls, Maria and Elizabeth, contract tuberculosis at school. Maria dies on May 6; Elizabeth dies June 15. Charlotte and Emily are withdrawn from the school on June 1. Charlotte and Emily do not return to school until they are in their teens; in the meantime they are educated at home.
1826   Reverend Brontë brings home a box of wooden soldiers for his son; this is the catalyst for the creation of the Brontës' juvenile fantasy worlds and writings. Charlotte and Branwell begin the "Angrian" stories and magazines; Emily and Anne work on the "Gondal" saga.
1831   Charlotte attends Miss Wooler's school. She leaves the school seven months later, to tend to her sisters' education. In 1835, however, she returns as governess. She is accompanied by Emily.
1835   After only three months, Emily leaves Miss Wooler's

	school because of homesickness. Anne arrives in January 1836 and remains until December 1837.
1837	In September, Emily becomes a governess at Miss Patchett's school, near Halifax.
1838	In May, Charlotte leaves her position at Miss Wooler's school.
1839	Anne becomes governess in the Ingram family at Blake Hall, Mirfield. She leaves in December. Charlotte becomes governess in the Sidwick family, at Stonegappe Hall, near Skipton. She leaves after two months (July).
1840	All three sisters live at Haworth.
1841	Anne becomes governess in the Robinson family, near York. Charlotte becomes governess in the White family and moves to Upperwood House, Rawdon. She leaves in December. The sisters plan to start their own school. The scheme, attempted several years later, fails for lack of inquiries.
1842	Charlotte and Emily travel to Brussels to study in the Pensionnat Héger. Here, Charlotte suffers unrequited love for the master of the school, M. Héger. Upon the death of their aunt in November, they return to Haworth.
1843	Branwell joins Anne in York as tutor to the Robinson family. Charlotte returns to Brussels and remains until January 1844.
1845	Charlotte discovers Emily's poetry and suggests that a selection be published along with the poetry of herself and Anne.
1846	*Poems, by Currer, Ellis, and Acton Bell* published by Aylott & Jones. Two copies are sold. Charlotte's *The Professor,* Emily's *Wuthering Heights,* and Anne's *Agnes Grey* are all completed. The latter two are accepted by T. C. Newby, but *The Professor* is rejected. Charlotte's *Jane Eyre* is begun in August and immediately accepted by Smith, Elder & Co. upon its completion in August 1847.
1847	*Jane Eyre* published. *Wuthering Heights* and *Agnes Grey* published by T. C. Newby.
1848	Anne's *The Tenant of Wildfell Hall* published by T. C. Newby, which tries to sell it to an American publisher as a new book by Currer Bell, author of the immensely popular *Jane Eyre.* Smith, Elder & Co. requests that Charlotte

bring her sisters to London to prove that there are three Bells. Charlotte and Anne visit London. Branwell dies of tuberculosis, September 24. Emily dies of the same, December 19.

1849   Anne dies of tuberculosis, May 28. Charlotte's *Shirley* published by Smith, Elder & Co. Charlotte meets Thackeray and Harriet Martineau in London.

1850   Charlotte meets G. H. Lewes and Mrs. Gaskell in London. Edits her sisters' work. Smith, Elder & Co. publish a new edition of *Wuthering Heights* and *Agnes Grey*, along with some of Anne's and Emily's poetry, and a "Biographical Notice" of her sisters' lives by Charlotte.

1852   The Reverend A. B. Nicholls proposes marriage to Charlotte. Her father objects, and Nicholls is rejected. Eventually, Reverend Brontë yields, and Charlotte marries in June 1854.

1853   Charlotte's *Villette* published in January.

1855   Charlotte dies of toxemia of pregnancy, March 31.

1857   Charlotte's *The Professor* published posthumously with a preface written by her husband. Mrs. Gaskell's *Life of Charlotte Brontë* published in March.

1860   "Emma," a fragment of a story by Charlotte, published in *The Cornhill Magazine* with an introduction by Thackeray.

1861   The Reverend Patrick Brontë, having survived all his children, dies.

Contributors

HAROLD BLOOM, Sterling Professor of the Humanities at Yale University, is the author of *The Anxiety of Influence, Poetry and Repression,* and many other volumes of literary criticism. A MacArthur Prize Fellow, he is general editor of five series of literary criticism published by Chelsea House.

W. A. CRAIK is Senior Lecturer at the University of Aberdeen and the author of *The Brontë Novels* and *Jane Austen: The Six Novels.*

BARBARA HARDY is Professor of English Literature at Birkbeck College at the University of London. Her publications include: *The Novels of George Eliot; The Moral Art of Dickens; A Reading of Jane Austen;* and, most recently, *Tellers and Listeners.*

TERRY EAGLETON, Lecturer at Oxford University, is the author of many books of criticism. His most recent publications include *The Rape of Clarissa: Writing, Sexuality, and Class Struggle in Richardson* and *Literary Theory: An Introduction.*

HELENE MOGLEN is Professor of English Literature and Dean of the Humanities and Arts at the University of California, Santa Cruz. She is the author of *Charlotte Brontë: The Self Conceived* and *The Philosophical Irony of Laurence Sterne.*

SANDRA M. GILBERT is Professor of English at Princeton University. SUSAN GUBAR is Professor of English at Indiana University. Together they have written *The Madwoman in the Attic* and edited *The Norton Anthology of Women's Literature* and *Shakespeare's Sisters: Feminist Essays on Women Poets.*

ROSEMARIE BODENHEIMER is Associate Professor of English at Boston College.

MARGARET HOMANS is Associate Professor of English at Yale University. Among her publications are *Women Writers and Poetic Identity: Dorothy Wordsworth, Emily Brontë, and Emily Dickinson* and *Bearing the Word: Language and Female Experience in Nineteenth-Century Women's Writing*.

Bibliography

Adams, Maurianne. "Family Disintegration and Creative Reinterpretation: The Case of Charlotte Brontë and *Jane Eyre*. In *The Victorian Family: Structure and Stresses,* edited by Anthony S. Wohl. New York: St. Martin's, 1976.

Allott, Miriam, ed. *The Brontës: The Critical Heritage.* London and Boston: Routledge & Kegan Paul, 1974.

Beaty, Jerome. "*Jane Eyre* and Genre." *Genre* 10, no. 1 (1977): 619–54.

Benvenuto, Richard. "The Child of Nature, the Child of Grace, and the Unresolved Conflict of *Jane Eyre*." *ELH* 39, no. 4 (December 1972): 620–38.

Blom, M. A. "Charlotte Brontë, Feminist Manquée." *Bucknell Review* 21, no. 1 (1973): 87–102.

———. "*Jane Eyre:* Mind as Law unto Itself." *Criticism* 15 (1973): 350–64.

Bloom, Harold, ed. *Modern Critical Views: The Brontës.* New Haven, Conn.: Chelsea House, 1986.

Burkhart, Charles. *Charlotte Brontë: A Psychosexual Study of Her Novels.* London: Victor Gollancz, 1973.

Cecil, David. *Victorian Novelists: Essays in Revaluation.* London: Constable, 1948.

Chase, Richard. "The Brontës, or, Myth Domesticated." In *Forms of Modern Fiction: Essays Collected in Honor of Joseph Warren Beach,* edited by William Van O'Connor, 102–19. Bloomington: Indiana University Press, 1962.

Cunningham, Valentine. *Everywhere Spoken Against: Dissent in the Victorian Novel.* Oxford: Clarendon Press, Oxford University Press, 1975.

Downing, Janay. "Fire and Ice Imagery in *Jane Eyre*." *Paunch* 26 (October 1966): 68–78.

Dunn, Richard J., ed. *Charlotte Brontë:* Jane Eyre. A Norton Critical Edition. New York: Norton, 1971.

Eriksen, Donald H. "Imagery as Structure in *Jane Eyre*." *Victorian Newsletter* 30 (Fall 1966): 18–22.

Ewbank, Inga-Stina. *Their Proper Sphere: A Study of the Brontë Sisters as Early-Victorian Female Novelists.* London: Edward Arnold, 1966.

Freeman, Janet H. "Speech and Silence in *Jane Eyre*." *Studies in English Literature 1500–1900* 24, no. 4 (Autumn 1984): 683–700.

Gaskell, Elizabeth. *The Life of Charlotte Brontë.* London: J. M. Dent, 1960.

Gerin, Winifred. *Charlotte Brontë: The Evolution of Genius.* Oxford: Oxford University Press, 1967.

Gregor, Ian, ed. *The Brontës: A Collection of Critical Essays.* Englewood Cliffs, N.J.: Prentice-Hall, 1970.

Grudin, Peter. "Jane and the Other Mrs. Rochester: Excess and Restraint in *Jane Eyre.*" *Novel* 10 (1977): 145–57.

Hagan, John. "Enemies of Freedom in *Jane Eyre.*" *Criticism* 13, no. 4 (Fall 1971): 351–76.

Heilbrun, Carolyn. *Toward a Recognition of Androgyny.* New York: Knopf, 1973.

Heilman, Robert B. "Charlotte Brontë, Reason, and the Moon." *Nineteenth-Century Fiction* 14, no. 4 (March 1960): 283–302.

———. "Charlotte Brontë's 'New' Gothic." In *From Jane Austen to Joseph Conrad,* edited by Robert C. Rathburn and Martin Steinmann, Jr., 118–32. Minneapolis: University of Minnesota Press, 1958.

Hinkley, Laura L. *The Brontës: Charlotte and Emily.* London: Hammond, 1947.

Horne, Margot. "From the Window-Seat to the Red Room: Innocence to Experience in *Jane Eyre.*" *Dutch Quarterly Review of Anglo-American Letters* 10 (1980): 199–213.

Kettle, Arnold. *An Introduction to the English Novel.* 2 vols. New York: Harper & Row, 1960.

Kiely, Robert. *The Romantic Novel in England.* Cambridge: Harvard University Press, 1972.

Knies, Earl. *The Art of Charlotte Brontë.* Athens: Ohio University Press, 1969.

Lenta, Margaret. "Jane Fairfax and Jane Eyre: Educating Women." *Ariel* 12, no. 4 (1981): 27–41.

Margoliath, Daniel. "Passion and Duty: A Study of Charlotte Brontë's *Jane Eyre.*" *Hebrew University Studies in Literature* 7 (1979): 182–213.

Martin, Robert. *The Accents of Persuasion: Charlotte Brontë's Novels.* London: Faber & Faber, 1966.

———. "*Jane Eyre* and the World of Faery." *Mosaic* 10, no. 4 (1977): 85–95.

Miller, J. Hillis. *The Form of Victorian Fiction.* Notre Dame, Ind.: University of Notre Dame Press, 1968.

Millgate, Jane. "Narrative Distance in *Jane Eyre:* The Relevance of the Pictures." *The Modern Language Review* 63, no. 2 (April 1968): 315–19.

Moglen, Helene. *Charlotte Brontë: The Self Conceived.* New York: Norton, 1976.

Ohmann, Carol. *Charlotte Brontë: The Limits of Her Feminism.* Old Westbury, N.Y.: Feminist Press, 1972.

Pell, Nancy. "Resistance, Rebellion, and Marriage: The Economics of *Jane Eyre.*" *Nineteenth-Century Fiction* 31, no. 4 (1977): 397–420.

Peters, Margot. *Charlotte Brontë: Style in the Novel.* Madison: University of Wisconsin Press, 1973.

———. *Unquiet Soul: A Biography of Charlotte Brontë.* New York: Doubleday, 1975.

Pinion, F. B. *A Brontë Companion: Literary Assessment, Background, and Reference.* London: Macmillan, 1975.

Ratchford, Fannie Elizabeth. *The Brontës' Web of Childhood.* New York: Columbia University Press, 1941.

Shannon, Edgar F., Jr. "The Present Tense in *Jane Eyre.*" *Nineteenth-Century Fiction* 10 (1956): 141–45.

Showalter, Elaine. *A Literature of Their Own: British Women Novelists from Brontë to Lessing.* Princeton: Princeton University Press, 1977.

Siebenschuh, William R. "The Image of the Child and the Plot of *Jane Eyre*." *Studies in the Novel* 8, no. 3 (Fall 1976): 304–17.

Sinclair, May. *The Three Brontës*. Boston and New York: Houghton Mifflin, 1912.

Sloman, Judith. "Jane Eyre's Childhood and Popular Children's Literature." In *Children's Literature* 3 (1974): 107–16.

Stone, Donald D. *The Romantic Impulse in Victorian Fiction*. Cambridge: Harvard University Press, 1980.

Tillotson, Kathleen. *Novels of the 1840s*. Oxford: Clarendon Press, Oxford University Press, 1954.

Winnifrith, Tom. *The Brontës and Their Background: Romance and Reality*. London: Macmillan, 1973.

Woolf, Virginia. "*Jane Eyre* and *Wuthering Heights*." In *Collected Essays*, vol. 1, 185–90. New York: Harcourt, Brace & World, 1967.

Yeazell, Ruth P. "More Truth than Real: Jane Eyre's 'Mysterious Summons.'" *Nineteenth-Century Fiction* 29, no. 2 (1974): 127–43.

Acknowledgments

"The Shape of the Novel" (originally entitled "Jane Eyre") by W. A. Craik from *The Brontë Novels* by W. A. Craik, © 1968 by W. A. Craik. Reprinted by permission of the author and Methuen & Co., Ltd.

"Providence Invoked: Dogmatic Form in *Jane Eyre* and *Robinson Crusoe*" (originally entitled "Dogmatic Form: Defoe, Charlotte Brontë, Thomas Hardy, and E. M. Forster") by Barbara Hardy from *The Appropriate Form: An Essay on the Novel* by Barbara Hardy, © 1964, 1970 by Barbara Hardy. Reprinted by permission.

"Jane Eyre: A Marxist Study" (originally entitled *"Jane Eyre"*) by Terry Eagleton from *Myths of Power: A Marxist Study of the Brontës,* © 1975 by Terry Eagleton. Reprinted by permission of Barnes & Noble Books, Totowa, New Jersey and by Macmillan Publishers Ltd.

"The End of *Jane Eyre* and the Creation of a Feminist Myth" (originally entitled *"Jane Eyre:* The Creation of a Feminist Myth") by Helene Moglen from *Charlotte Brontë: The Self Conceived* by Helene Moglen, © 1976 by Helene Moglen. Reprinted by permission of the author and the University of Wisconsin Press. The notes have been omitted.

"A Dialogue of Self and Soul: Plain Jane's Progress" by Sandra M. Gilbert and Susan Gubar from *The Madwoman in the Attic: The Woman Writer and the Nineteenth-Century Literary Imagination* by Sandra M. Gilbert and Susan Gubar, © 1979 by Yale University. Reprinted by permission of Yale University Press.

"Jane Eyre in Search of Her Story" by Rosemarie Bodenheimer from *Papers on Language and Literature* 16, no. 4 (Fall 1980), © 1980 by the Board of Trustees, Southern Illinois University. Reprinted by permission.

"Dreaming of Children: Literalization in *Jane Eyre*" by Margaret Homans from *Bearing the Word: Language and Female Experience in Nineteenth-Century Women's Writing* by Margaret Homans, © 1986 by the University of Chicago. Reprinted by permission of the University of Chicago Press. This essay originally appeared in *Female Gothic,* edited by Juliann E. Fleenor. © 1983 by Eden Press. Reprinted by permission.

143

.

Index

Adam Bede (George Eliot), 88
Agnes Grey (Anne Brontë), 1
Algren, Nelson, 2
Alienation, as theme, 60
Angrian legend, 6, 24, 63, 73
"Anybody may blame me who likes," 74–75
Art: and audience, 101; and credibility, 103
Austen, Jane, 2, 19

Bible, The, 6, 89–90
Blake, William, 2
Borderers, The (Wordsworth), 2
Brocklehurst, Mr., 30, 34, 53, 56, 60, 99; as captor, 91, hypocrisy of, 82; Jane's humiliation by, 68; stinginess of, 71; as symbol of patriarchy, 91; as Victorian superego, 70, 71
Brontë, Anne: as model for Mary Rivers, 50; writings of, 1
Brontë, Branwell, 52
Brontë, Charlotte: Matthew Arnold on, 64; attitude toward conventional fiction of, 106; attitude toward passion of, 30; and Branwell Brontë, 52, 58; and Emily Brontë, 30, 113; class bias of, 51; and death of mother, 118; and Emily Dickinson, 87; as family benefactor, 52; and father, 58, 59; feminism of, 51, 60, 94; on Gothic novel, 116; idioms used by, 18–19; influence of Byron on, 3, 4; influence of Thackeray on, 19; and male sexuality, 53, 93; marriage to Arthur

Bell Nicolls, 21; motivation to write of, 95; Anne Mozley on, 64; mythic elements of, 77; on the novel, 20; optimism of, 95; political ambiguity of, 19; as realist novelist, 23; Elizabeth Rigby on, 64; Romanticism in work of, 35; "self-possession" of, 38; sexual panic of, 81; style of, 15–16, 19; view of male role of, 80. *See also* Jane Eyre; Romantic ethos; Sexuality, male
Brontë, Emily: and Anne Brontë, 1; and Charlotte Brontë, 30; conventionality of, 30; as Gothic novelist, 116; as mentor, 50; as model for Diana Rivers, 50; use of dialect by, 18; use of metaphor by, 129; views on childbirth of, 114
Brontë, Patrick, 58, 59
Brontë sisters: as creators of new fiction genre, 1; as governesses, 30; obsession with male sexuality of, 77
Bunyan, John, 49, 63–64, 68, 69, 94
Burns, Helen: as antecedent for St. John Rivers, 52–53, 90; as antithesis to Jane, 48; death of, 24; friendship of, 9; as Jane's critic, 100; and Jane's expectations, 22; on love, 25; as mother figure, 73; as romantic conservative, 29; as saint, 76; significance of name of, 72; stoicism of, 72, 105; as voice of Charlotte Brontë, 27, 72
Byron, George Gordon, Lord, 5, 6, 59–60, 73; as antecedent of Charlotte Brontë, 3; as cult figure, 2; as paradigmatic hero, 1–2; as proto-